GUIDE TO UNDERSTANDING THE HOLY QUR-AN

BY: THE MOST HONORABLE

MR. ELIJAH MUHAMMAD

NWNOI Publications

PO Box 8466

Newark, NJ 07108

www.nwnoi.org

Library of Congress Cataloging-In-Publication Data:

Guide To Understanding the Holy Qur-an

Hardcover ISBN: 978-1-970854-12-1

Paperback ISBN: 978-1-970854-15-2

E-Book ISBN: 978-1-970854-13-8

Audiobook ISBN: 978-1-970854-14-5

Religion / Islam / General

Religion / Spirituality/ General

Religion / Comparative Religion

Religion / Qur-anic Studies / General

Social Sciences / Ethnic Studies/African American Studies

Social Science / Black Studies (Global)

History / African American & Black Studies

Philosophy / Religious

Theology / Liberation Theology

Cultural Studies / African American Religion and Spirituality

Creative Direction & Layout by

Art Supplied Gfx

www.artdiggs.com

Printed in USA

A Tribute of
Gratitude and Excellence

I extend my deepest gratitude to the **New World Nation of Islam FOI** and the following sisters for their contributions:

- **Sister AC Ukht Hadiyah Muhammad**
- **Sister Muqarabun Ali**

A special thank you to **Alah Adams** for the meticulous proofreading.

Your dedication and excellence to this great work are truly apprcciated.

- **Sister FSC Mutadirah Ali**

This guide is only the beginning. For those who wish to absorb these teachings more deeply, an ***audiobook version of Guide to Understanding the Holy Quran*** *is available. Listen anytime, anywhere, and let the wisdom unfold with you on the go.*

www.nwnoimedia.com

GUIDE TO UNDERSTANDING THE HOLY QUR-AN

Table of Contents

Chapter 1

Holy Qur-an 72: 8-9

A Flame Lying in Wait for Him

> 72:8 *And we sought to reach heaven, but we found it filled with strong guards and flames:*
>
> 72:9 *And we used to sit in some of the sitting places thereof to steal a hearing. But he who tries to listen now finds a flame lying in wait for him:*

She holds a whole nation (so-called Negroes) prisoner, and refuses to open the door of freedom, justice and equality to them. She threatens to go to war against other nations who held any of her citizens prisoners. They now boast of building rockets to land on our moon (which can't and won't be done); and to build a small contraption to try circling the earth like our moon, which we have made to revolve around the earth.

The following is from the Holy Qur-an: "And we (the devils) sought to reach heaven, but we found it filled with strong guards and flames and we (the devils) used to sit in some of the sitting places thereof to steal a hearing. But he who tries to listen now finds a flame lying in wait for him." (Holy Qur-an 72: 8, 9)

I am for the separation of my people from their enemies; that they share not in the enemies' destruction even though I may lose my own life in this daring attempt to save them by the plain, simple truth of God and power. It must be done and will be done, regardless of who or what. It can be done in one day but Allah desires to make Himself known in the West, as it is written of Him. ***(MTBM pg. 110)***

Holy Qur-an 30:30

A Muslim is not a Muslim Unless

> *30:30 So set they face for religion, being upright the nature made by Allah, in which He has created men. There is no altering Allah's creation. That is the right religion but most people know not*

Why should we be looking and begging for that which is good (freedom, justice and equality)! Islam is that right religion (which by nature they cannot give us.)

According to the Holy Qur-an (30:30), one of the greatest teachings of brotherhood is laid down by us by the Prophet Muhammad in these words: "A Muslim is not a Muslim until he loves for his brother what he loves for himself." The old Christian religion has been the white man's whip to lash the black man ever since it was organized. My people here in America are fast awakening to the slavery teachings of Christ vanity to the dislike of their enemies.

A few years ago the so-called Negroes could easily be frightened and worked up into emotion by the preachers, yelling and spitting out foam all over the pulpit, preaching hellfire after death and the dying of Jesus on the cross. He would paint an imaginary picture in the minds of the listeners of meeting some dead relative up in the heavens (sky) after death or mourn them into grief and sorrow. My people are leaving, rejecting such nonsense as they advance more and more educationally. After they have heard the truth of it all, that Allah has and is teaching me, they will not go near that slavery teaching. Their eyes must be opened to the truth at any price. ***(MTBM pgs. 79-80)***

Holy Qur-an 10:25

Abode of Peace

> 10:25 *And Allah invites to the abode of peace, guides whom He pleases to the right path.*

Allah invites to the abode of peace (Holy Qur-an 10:25). Can you imagine a divine prophet being sent with anything other than a religion of peace to his people?

Our people, the so-called American Negroes, will love Islam when they learn more of it. For it is the religion of their fathers, and it is the last of the three great religions on earth. The other two, Buddhism and Christianity, cannot give us a lasting peace. We have tried them to our disappointment.

Christianity is one of the most perfect black slave-making religions on our planet. It has completely killed the so-called Negroes mentally.

Now it takes Allah (God) Himself to revive and restore our people back into their own. Though I am His messenger, and Allah can use my life as He pleases for them, they are my people and many while I am only one.

Islam will give them the heaven while they live. Islam has more to offer than the white controlled Christianity. Islam is universal. The true believers of Islam are equal in number to the total population of the whites on our planet (400 million).

By nature, all members of the black nation are Muslims (lovers of peace), whose number is over the billion mark.

We must have Islam as our religion to restore our peace after suffering under the slavery, the persecutions, and the grievous of wars for 6000 years. The so-called Negroes of America, who have never known the way of peace, who have never had love or mercy shown to them, today have Allah (God). ***(MTBM pg. 70)***

Holy Qur-an 13:32

All Messengers attacked by disbelievers and government of their time

13:32 And messengers before thee were certainly mocked, but I gave respite to those who disbelieved. Then I seized them. How (awful) was then my requital."

Many of the Orthodox Muslims do not want to believe that Allah has appeared in the Person of Master Fard Muhammad or that He has made manifest the truth that has been hidden from their religious scientist the truth of God and of the devil as revealed to me. Though they do have the Holy Qur-an, many of them do not understand the meaning of it and some of them believe everything that is prophesied in the Bible and Holy Qur-an, many of them do not understand the meaning of it. And some of them believe everything that is prophesied in the Bible and Holy Qur-an about a last Messenger or Prophet being or referring to Muhammad of 1400 years ago.

They even take all of the people prophesied from Moses to Jesus, who received a prophet coming after Moses and like Moses to the people of Mohammad of 1400 years ago. This is very wrong. It must be understood that the prophesies are referring to God and a Messenger in the resurrection of the dead in the last years of this world ruled by the Caucasian people.

Moses and Jesus were both examples of what not the end of Moses and Jesus world. Moses and Jesus lives were examples of what would take place among the so-called Negro in America that lost and found people mentioned so much by Jesus in Revelations where it is shown that the Messenger becomes a lamb.

In Revelations, the symbolic land is in the midst of four symbolic beasts. All of the scholars and scientist of the white race know this is not referring to Muhammad of 1400 years ago.

The anger of the beasts refers to a dragon against the Messenger who is referred to as a lamb or as a woman pregnant with child. This is one of the clearest prophesies of the opposition against him in the last days and the type of people to whom the revelation refused to give credit for being not human beings but beasts who desire to destroy the woman and her child.

This only means the Messenger and his followers of Islam.

All messengers were attacked by disbelievers and governments of their time, according to the Quaran. As an example of what the last Messenger and his followers would face, Pharaoh openly confessed that he desired to slay Moses and did not believe that God (Allah) would be able to protect Moses from his evil plans.

But the Holy Qur-an says that Allah made him an example, for in the last days both Moses and the symbolic lamb are declared to be victorious.

Revelations states that the lamb and his followers, after escaping the evil plans of the beast, sang the song of Moses, which was of the victory over Pharaoh.

Let us remember that the scholars and scientist have not understood the two interpretations of the Bible and Holy Qur-an concerning the last messenger. They should meet and confess on this most important of all scripture and come to the correct interpretation.

Both of you, Christians and Orthodox Muslims, are absolutely wrong to believe all of this prophecy refers to Jesus or Moses and a prophet like himself and to believe that the symbolic lamb in Revelation refers to Jesus or Moses and a prophet like himself and to believe that the symbolic lamb in Revelation refers to Jesus or, as the Orthodox Muslims believe, that it refers to Muhammad of 1400 years ago. How gravely you must interpret your Bible and Holy Qur-an. This important understanding is causing a lot of division.

Some of the well-read scholars among the Orthodox Muslims are grieves to hear from America that I call myself a Messenger of Allah, though not one of them has been able to do the work that I have done in resurrecting my people in America. They could not do it. It was not for them to do what I am doing (the resurrecting of the dead.) Their own Holy Qur-an teaches them that Allah teaches a Messenger from every people that he intended to warn or destroy. It tells them in plan words that an Arab and an Arabic Holy Qur-an could not be the instrument sent to the people who must be resurrected because they would have the excuse that they could not read Arabic and therefore exercise their disbelief by saying that this was an Arab and an Arabic Qur-an. **(MTBM pgs. 188-189)**

Holy Qur-an 2:1

Allah, Best Knower

2:1 *I, Allah, am the best Knower.*

There are many other chapters of the Holy Qur-an Sharrieff that open with the above words, "Allah is the best Knower." The beautiful teachings of the Holy Qur-an have no equal in other scriptures.

All so-called Negro preachers should have one but be sure it is the one translated by Yusuf Ali, or Malvi Muhammad Ali. Any other translation of the Holy Qur-an, by Christian authors, is as poisonous to the reader as a rattle snake.

What I am trying to make clear is that white people do not believe in Allah and Islam or the prophets of Allah. Why then, should you seek the truth of it from them? You will soon come to know that you should not seek any truth from them. They have you following in the wrong direction and hope to keep you like that; but by my Allah's power and wisdom, and my life's blood, you shall know the truth even against your own will.

Holy Qur-an 4:107

Allah does not have him who is treacherous

> 4:107 *And content not on behalf of those who act unfaithfully to their souls. Surely Allah loves not him who is treacherous, sinful.*

A hypocrite, regardless to where he appears or regardless to what ogrganization he may be a member of whether a governmental hypocrite, an industrial hypocrite, a business hypocrite or a religious hypocrite is the most unwanted and hated of all the people concerned They are also the most hated by God. They are double-crossers; they come in claiming belief and then go out disbelieving.

I quote several passages of the Holy Qur-an on hypocrites of which the average leader or searcher of the scripture has not known, because the scripture teachers here in America have never studied the Holy Qur-an. If they had, they would not be hard to awaken or be united with their own kind.

In section 16, entitled "Hypocrites are Dishonest," the Muslims are warned not to try to defend them or contend on behalf of those who act unfaithfully to their souls. "Surely Allah loves not him who is treacherous, sinful." (4:107) ***(MTBM pg. 255)***

Holy Qur-an 3:31

Allah does not love disbelievers

> 3:31*"Say: Obey Allah and the Messenger; but if they turn back, Allah surely loves not the disbelievers."*

The religion of Islam demands strict obedience to Allah and His Messenger. The word "Islam" means submission "obedience". Obedience to God (Allah) is not accepted if one is disobedient to the Messenger. ***(MTBM pg. 259)***

SECTION 2 Progress of the Faithful

Holy Qur-an 112:1-4

Allah is One

112:1 Say: He, Allah, is One.

112:1 Allah is He on whom all depend.

112:3 He begets not, nor is. He begotten.

112:4 And none is like Him.

Islam, Only True Religion of God

A Muslim is one who believes in One God. It is forbidden by Allah (God) for us to believe in or serve anyone other than Himself as a god. He warns us not to set up an equal with Him, as He was the one in the beginning from whom everything had its beginning and will be the One God from which everything will end. He is independent, having no need of anyone's help, but on the other hand, upon Him we all depend. It is the highest of ignorance for us to choose a God or attempt to make something as an equal to Him. Foolish people all over the earth have been for the past 6000 years, and still are, trying to make an equal to Allah (God). He has no beginning, nor is there any end of Him. How, O foolish man, can you make an equal for such a One? How foolish we make ourselves, serving and worshipping gods other than the One God, Allah.

The foolish become rich and highly educated in their way and not in the way of Allah and then begin making and worshiping gods of their own, the work of their own hands then comes the end of them as it is of today.

It is the fundamental principle of the religion of Islam to believe in Allah, the One God, According to the belief, the teaching and preaching of the prophets of Allah is of One God. Noah, Abraham, Moses, and Jesus -- all believe in One God (Allah). The Christians claim a belief in the above-named prophets -- then how do they make Jesus the equal of Allah (God)? The Bible says, and God spoke all these words saying: "I am the Lord, thy God, thou shalt have no other gods before Me. Thou shalt not make unto thee any graven image, or any likeness of anything that is in the heavens above, or that is in the earth beneath, or that is in the water under the earth; thou shalt not bow down thyself to them, nor serve them, for I, the Lord Thy God, am a jealous God."

Both Jews and Christians are guilty of setting up rivals to Allah (God). Adam and Eve accepted the guidance of the serpent instead of that of Allah (Gen. 3:6). They made a golden calf and took it for their god and bowed down to it (Exod. 32:4). This was the work of their own hands to guide them and fight their wars. The Christians have made imaginary pictures and statues of wood, silver and gold -- calling them pictures and statues of God. They bow down to pictures and statues alleged to be of Jesus, His mother, and his disciples as though they could see and hear them. They (the Christians) claim sonship to Allah (God) and take the Son to be the equal of the Father, though they say "that they killed the Son." Today they take the weapons of war for their gods and put their trust in the work of their own hands.

Muhammad took hold of the best, the belief in one God (Allah), and was successful. Fourteen hundred years after him, we are successful, that is, we who will not set up another god with Allah. The fools who refuse to believe in Allah alone as the One God, if asked who made heaven and earth, most surely would say God and would say God the Son and the Holy Ghost. Then why do they not serve and obey Allah (God)?

It is a perfect insult to Allah (God) who made heaven and earth and makes the earth to produce everything for our service and even the sun, moon, and stars -- they serve our needs -- for us to bow down and worship anything other than Allah as a god. The Great Mahdi, Allah in person, who is in our midst today, will put a stop once and forever to the serving and worshiping of other gods besides Himself.

It is the devil's way of bringing the people (so-called Negroes) of Allah (God) in opposition to Him by teaching the people to believe and do just the thing that God forbids. Muhammad did not try making a likeness of God, nor have his followers done that. He and his followers obey the law of (the one God) Allah, while the Jews and the Christians preach it and do otherwise. We are now being brought face to face with Allah (God) for a showdown between Him and that which we have served as God besides Him. The lost and found members of the Asiatic nation are especially warned in the 112th chapter of the Holy Qur-an against the worship of any other god than Allah, for it is Allah in person who has found them among the worshipers of gods other than Allah. ***(MTBM pgs. 73-75)***

Holy Qur-an 40:2

Allah, The Mighty, Knowing

40:2 The revelation of the Book is from Allah, the Mighty, the Knowing.

The book that the so-called American Negroes (Tribe of Shabazz) should own and read, the book that the slave-masters have, but have not represented it to their slaves, is a book that will heal their sin-sick souls that were made sick and sorrowful by the slave-masters. The book will open their blinded eyes and open their deaf ears. The book that will purify them, the book that makes a distinction between the God of righteousness and the God of evil, the book of guidance, the book of light and truth, the book of wisdom and judgement.

But the average one should first be taught how to respect such as a book, how to read it, how to understand it, how to teach it. The Holy Qur-an Sharrieff contains some of the most beautiful prayers that one ever heard recited or read. It is called the Glorious Qur-an and without mistake that is just what it is. This book is not from a prophet, but direct from Allah to Muhammad, not by an angel, but from the mouth of Allah (God). The great distinguisher between truth and falsehood in the judgment of the world, of whom the enemy of truth has ruled the nation of black mankind with falsehood for the past six thousand years.

This book pulls the cover off the covered and shows the nation for the first time that which deceived 90 percent of the people of the earth without the knowledge of the deceiver. The revelation of the book is from Allah, The Mighty, The Knowing (Chapt. 40:2), according to the above chapter and second verse. Allah is The Mighty, One over all other beings, and is the Knowing One. Therefore, He Knows what is best for every living thing. And the book (Qur-an) that he has revealed there is no doubt about it, for the All Knowing One, the Best Knower has revealed it: One who has no equal, the All wise. ***(MTBM pg. 92)***

Chapter 2

Holy Qur-an 4:140, 142, 145, 138

Allah will gather hypocrites, disbelievers

> 4:140 *And indeed He has revealed it to you in the Book that when you hear Allah's messages disbelieved in and mocked at, sit not with them until they enter into some other discourse, for then indeed you would be like them. Surely Allah will gather together the hypocrites and the disbelievers all in hell.*
>
> 4:142 *The hypocrites seek to deceive Allah, and He will requite their deceit to them. And when they stand up for prayer, they stand up sluggishly they do it only to be seen of men and remember Allah but little,*
>
> 4:145 *The hypocrites are surely in the lowest depths of the fire, and thou wilt find no helper for them*
>
> 4:138 *Give news to the hypocrites that for them is a painful chastisement.*

The Holy Qur-an has the same announcement for all disbelievers and hypocrites of the messenger. It is also the same given to Noah and his followers. It is the same given to all disbelieving foes and hypocrites. The hypocrites around Moses, Jesus and Muhammad were given the same warnings. And they, (the hypocrites) are prophesied in the Holy Qur-an (which is a very true book), to be the same type of hypocrites and to be saying the same words to the last Apostle and his true followers today as they did to the former prophets and their followers.

My followers here in America and the hypocrites among them are now being manifested to be the same as all others in the past. The hypocrites utter the same words, make mockery of the Messenger and his followers, and plan to do harm to us just as the hypocrites of the past did all other Messengers and their followers.

A hypocrite is one who first says he believes in Islam and then disbelieves and seeks to oppose the messenger and those who believe in him and his God. Their punishment says the Holy Qur-an in several places is grief, regret, shame and disgrace. ***(MTBM pg. 260-261)***

Holy Qur-an 2:15

Allah will pay back the hypocrite

> 2:15 *Allah will pay them back their mockery, and He leaves them alone in their inordinacy, friendly wandering on.*

A hypocrite is a person who is disliked by everyone whether it be a hypocritical wife, husband, parent, son or daughter, the hypocrite is unwanted. You can never trust hypocrites. They are liars. They are worse than disbelievers, because a disbeliever has not lied, saying that he believed and then turned back. This makes hypocrites the most hated of all people.

When they come in, they hope to make Allah think that they are believers and, on their leaving, sincerely seek to deceive the true believers so that they may turn them against Allah, the Messenger, and the truth that he has brought. They are mockers of the believers and say that they believe but yet they are mockers of true believers. ***(MTBM pg. 252)***

Holy Qur-an 61:8

Allah will perfect His light

> 61:8 *They desire to put out the light of Allah with their mouths, but Allah will perfect His light, though the disbelievers may be averse.*

They desire to put out the light of Allah with their mouths, but Allah will perfect His light though the unbelievers may be averse. Regardless of the opponents' efforts to put out the light of truth (Islam) today, their efforts will be a complete failure. Think over the slavery teachings of Christianity the three gods, the worship of Mary, the disciples of Jesus, the many gods of Buddhism, the incarnation taught by both and other ignorant practices. Islam teaches an eternal heaven for the righteous, for hell is not eternal.

These (heaven and hell) are not necessary places but conditions. Islam teaches that if a brother kills a brother, the murderer must be killed, or anyone that murders a Muslim.

The Christians go to war against each other daily, killing their own brothers and others. The righteous must be rid of such people. Make Islam to overcome all other religions whether the disbelievers like it or not. Our God is one God. Can One God believe in more than one religion and be true to Himself and others? ***(MTBM pg. 76)***

Holy Qur-an 47:33-34

Allah will not forgive those who hinder

> *47:33 O you who believe, obey Allah and obey the Messenger, and make not your deeds in vain.*
>
> *47:34 Surely those who disbelieve and hinder (men) from Allah's way then die disbelievers, Allah will not forgive them.*

Allah will chastise Messengers if they disobey Him, but Allah does not allow us to be the judge of His Messengers, nor does He make a second choice in chopping a Messenger for another. Read the histories of the Prophets of God.

God is very hard on those who disobey His Messenger. He warns in His Holy Qur-an not to quarrel and dispute or raise our voices above the Messenger's voice. Strict respect and honor is demanded for His Messengers. We should not take them lightly.

We may underestimate them without knowledge. (MTBM pg. 260)

Holy Qur-an 44:10

America in for trouble

> 44:10 *So wait for the day when the heaven brings a clear drought.*

Just why do you want to be like the people who have robbed, spoiled and slain you and your fathers? Is it not an act of intelligence and honor to desire to look and be like a member of your own nation, speaking the same language and seeking and building the culture of your kind? This white race wants to stay a white race and maintain its way of life. Why should we not want to do the same?

You may say, what is our nation's way of life? I will admit that for the past few centuries you have been lost to the knowledge of self and kind. Allah has raised me to teach you the knowledge of your own self and kind and to join you onto your own kind, not as a subjected people. For superior wisdom cannot be subjected to inferior wisdom. And, a people guided by Allah, Himself cannot be enslaved.

You must know the outlook and what must be done. America is in for much trouble as the Holy Qur-an says: "One calamity followed by another until she is destroyed for her evils done to her slaves."

These calamities consist of all sorts of confusion and disagreements between the people and the heads of governments. In the Bible and the Holy Qur-an, revolutions and wars are mentioned as being forced to break the power of resistance. The Bible says: "Sword without and sword within. The forces of nature against a terrific drought prophesied." In the Holy Qur-an it says: "Therefore, keep waiting for the day when the heaven shall bring a clean drought, that shall overtake men. This is a painful chastisement." *(MTBM pg. 302-303)*

Holy Qur-an 4:103

Be Steadfast in Prayer

4:103 So when you have finished the prayer, remember Allah standing and sitting and reclining. But when you are secure, from danger, keep up (regular) prayer. Prayer indeed has been enjoined on the believers at fixed times.

"That which leads man to infidelity is neglect of prayers."

"No one of you must say his prayers in a garment without covering the whole body."

"Allah accepts not the prayers of a woman arrived at puberty unless she covers her head as well as the whole body."

"The five stated prayers erase the sins which have been committed during the intervals between them if they have not been mortal sins."

"The prayers of a person will not be accepted, who has broken his ablution until he completes another ablution."

"Order your children to say the state prayer when they are seven years of age, and beat them if they do not do so when they are ten years old."

"Tell me if any one of you had a rivulet before his doors and bathed five times a day therein whether any dirt would remain on his body? The companions said "Nothing would remain! The Prophet said, 'In this manner will the five daily prayers as ordered' by Allah erase all minor sins."

The lost-found joins the righteous in prayer for the first time upon their finding by Allah.

We see him turning himself to Allah to recite the prayer of the righteous. The presence of Allah is like the sun in all its brilliance on him in the early morning after a long dreary night and his first thought was to rise up and prepare for the day. *(MTBM pgs. 143-144)*

Holy Qur-an 5:8

Be Steadfast in the Cause of Allah

> 5:8 *O you who believe, be upright for Allah, bearers of witness with justice; and let not hatred of a people incite you not to act equitably. Be just that is nearer to observance of duty. And keep your duty to Allah. Surely Allah is aware of what you do.*

We owe our very lives to Allah, the Lord of all the worlds. Why should we not thank Him? Or every good thought we owe to Allah, the beneficent, the merciful. Surely as often as we sin, we turn to Him in prayer. He is most merciful and grants us pardon and oftentimes we drift back again to some other flaw. For this we must turn to Him again, asking to be forgiven surely Allah knows what is in our hearts, and what is more, he is oft-forgiving. *(MTBM pg. 135-136)*

Holy Qur-an 20:14

Best remembrance of Allah through prayer

> 20:14 *Surely I am Allah, there is no God but I, so serve Me and keep up prayer for my remembrance.*

He, who is the All Perfect One, who knows our imperfection and pardons most through His messenger. Remember: And the best way for remembrance of Allah (God) is through prayer.

The five prayers of the day are spiritual refreshments and he who cleanses himself in and out leaves no faithfulness. It would be an insult to invite His Lord's holy spirit into a house the outside of which was filthy.

Why should we not pray five times a day to our Maker since we feed our bodies 3 times a day? What is so important that would keep us away from prayer to the Originator of the heavens and the earth?

Let us give praises to our God and submit ourselves to the Lord of the worlds and learn how to pray the right prayers in the right manner. Let us serve One True God, whose proper name is Allah, in the right state.

"My Lord, make me to keep up prayer and my offspring too. Our Lord, accept the prayer. Our Lord, grant Thy protection to me and to my parents and to the faithful on the day when the reckoning will be taken." (The prayer of the Muslims will get you an answer!) ***(MTBM pg. 136)***

Holy Qur-an 68:10-16

Beware of hypocrites

68:10 *And obey not any mean swearer*

68:11 *Defamer going about slander*

68:12 *Hinderer of good, outstepping the limits, sinful*

68:13 *Ignoble, besides all that, notoriously mischievous*

68:14 *Because he possesses wealth and sons.*

68:15 *When Our messages are recited to him, he says: Stories of those of yore!*

68:16 *We shall brand him on the snout.*

All the mighty men of science and modern warfare have been called in an effort to devise instruments and weapons against God and the armies of heaven. The nations of the earth are angry. The disbelievers and hypocrites of my people also are angry over the change of the old world to a new world of justice and righteousness, causing much spiritual darkness and misunderstanding to fall upon them. They want to judge the person Allah should. Choose for His Messenger.

Believers, be aware of this chief hypocrite who has, for the past year, stepped beyond the limits in trying to keep people from following me (see Holy Qur-an 68:10-16)

I am no more to suffer the evil and slanderous talk of the disbelievers (as though they are the judges of Allah's messenger) as did the Messenger before me. Not one of you of the 22 million who do not believe in the truth that I am teaching will harm me in the very least' you are harming only yourselves. As I have said, Allah has given me the key to your mental death here in America (hell). I am not allowed by Him to even beg you to believe, because the truth is plain enough for a fool to see and say that it is the truth. *(MTBM pg. 269)*

Holy Qur-an 15:28

Black mud fashioned into shape

> 15:28*And when the Lord said to the angels: I am going to create a mental sounding clay, of black mud fashioned into shape.*

Your Lord said to the angels, "Surely I am going to create a mortal of essence of black mud fashioned in shape."

The essence of black mud (the black nation) mentioned is only symbolic, which actually means the sperm of the black nation, and they refused to recognize the black nation as their equal though they were made from and by a black scientist (named Yakub). They can never see their way in submitting to Allah and the religion Islam and His prophets. *(MTBM pg. 128)*

Holy Qur-an 20:130

Celebrate the praise of Lord

> 20:130 *So bear patiently what they say, and celebrate the praise of thy Lord before the rising of the sun and before its setting, and glorify (Him) during the hours of the night and parts of the day, that though mayest be well pleased.*

The presence of Allah is like the sun in all its brilliance on him in the early morning after a long dreary night and his first thought was to rise up and prepare for the day. ***(MTBM pg. 143)***

Holy Qur-an 5:3

Chosen for your, Islam

> *5:3 Forbidden to you is that which dies of itself, and blood, and flesh of swine, and that on which any other name than that of Allah has been invoked, and the strangled (animal) and that beaten to death, and that killed by a fall and that killed by being smitten with the horn, and that which wild beasts have eaten, except what you slaughter, and what is sacrificed on stones set up (for idols) and that you divide by the arrows; that is a transgression. This day have those who disbelieve despaired of your religion, so fear them not, and fear Me. This day have I perfected for you your religion and completed My favor on you and chosen for you Islam as a religion; but whoever is compelled by hunger, not inclining willfully to sin, then surely Allah is Forgiving, Merciful.*

What is Islam? It can be answered in one word righteousness. Briefly, it is the religion of Allah (God) and His Prophets. Islam is as old as Allah (God) Himself and is the religion of which Allah (God) is the author. Islam is the religion of Adam, Noah, Moses, Jesus, and Muhammad (the last). Islam is the religion of entire submission to the will of Allah (God). Islam is the religion which the Holy Qur-an teaches.

Allah (God) says, "This day I have perfected for you your religion, completed my favor on you and chosen for you, Islam as a religion." Allah (God) also says in another chapter of the holy Qur-an, "Surely the true religion with Allah is Islam" (3:18).

The significance of the name "Islam" is peace, the true religion. It is a religion of eternal peace. We cannot imagine Allah

(God) offering to us a religion other than one of peace. A religion of peace coming to the righteous after the destruction of the wicked is also mentioned in several places in the Bible: "The Lord will bless his people with peace," (Psa. 29:11) also "He will speak peace unto His people and to His saints" (Psa. 85:8) and "the Lord of peace give you peace always" (II Thess. 3:16) *(MTBM pg. 69)*

Holy Qur-an 30:41

Corruption has appeared in the Land

> 30:41 *Corruption has appeared in the land and the sea on account of that which men's hands have wrought, that He may make them taste a part of that which they have done, so that they may return.*

ON UNIVERSAL CORRUPTION

Allah, the All Wise, the Best Knower, who has knowledge of the past the present and the future revealed this above prophecy to Muhammad (May the peace and blessings of Allah be upon him) nearly 1400 years ago, as though it were taking place during that time. However, it was referring to these days, and we see the manifestation and fulfillment of the above verse.

There is no doubt in anyone's mind today that the condition of the nations is such that it needs a ruler who is not involved in the present world of corruption to bring about peace and goodwill among the people of the earth. There cannot be peace until the peace breakers have been removed from authority and their activities of mischief making, causing bloodshed, grief, sorrow and trouble among peace-loving nations.

There is not a civilized government of people at this writing that is not in trouble and trying to find a solution to the cause. All the nations of the earth are so corrupt with other than good that they cannot come to any agreement on peace with each other, they carry it into practice. The disagreement and corruption today is seen not only in the Christian world of Europe and America but also in the very heart of the Holy Land in Africa and Asia.

Corruption started in Europe, and it has now spread over nine-tenths of the population of the Planet Earth. It has caused the dissatisfaction of nearly 100 per cent of the civilized nations.

Dissatisfaction has reached such a percentage that it is bound to bring about universal war, since the corruption is universal. The continuing disagreement between the heads of the nations is referred to as CONFUSED and CONFLICT in the Bible and Holy Qur-an. In this world of universal corruption and crises and the ever-growing threat of universal war, we, the so- called American Negroes, the Lost-Found members of the tribe Shabazz, should unite and take our stand on the side of Allah (God), His religion of peace (Islam) and our own nation (the Black People). ***(MTBM pg. 265-266)***

Chapter 3

Holy Qur-an 76:2

Created man from sperm

> *76:2 Surely we have created man from sperm mixed (with ovum), to thy him, so We have made him hearing, seeing.*

Just what have we learned, or rather are learning from this divine revelation of our enemies, the devils? Answer: We are learning the truth which has been kept a secret for 6000 years concerning the white race, who have deceived us. WE learn what is meant by the Bible's symbolic teachings: that they were made from dust.

This only tends to convey the idea that they were created from nothing; which means the low and humble origin of such creation.

Again, we learn who the Bible (Genesis 1:26) is referring to in the saying: "Let us make man." This "US" was fifty-nine thousand nine hundred and ninety-nine (59,999) black men and women; making or grafting them into the likeness or image of the original man.

Not that they are the same, but have the ways of a human being they are referred to as "mankind" not the real original man, but a being made like the original in the sense of human beings.

The Holy Qur-an throws a great light on the truth of the creation of this pale, white race of devils. "O mankind, surely we have created you from a male and a female."

(Chap. 49:15) This makes it very easy to understand to whom it is referring. "What mankind?" Surely we created man from sperm mixed (with ovum) to try him, so we have made him hearing and seeing" (Chap 76:2).

In as much as these chapters have a further reference to the spiritual creation of the Last Messenger, it is equally true that they refer to the physical creation of the White race. In another place, the Holy Qur-an says: "We have created man, and now he is an open disputer." ***(MTBM pgs. 118-119)***

Holy Qur-an 45:14

Days of Allah

> *45:14 Tell those who believe to forgive those who fear not the days of Allah that He may reward a people for what they earn.*

The Days of Allah

What is meant by "Days of Allah" are the battles between right and wrong. They are often mentioned as follows: the Days of Judgment, the Days of resurrection, the Days of the Son of Man, and the Days of Allah. These days must not be mistaken for the regular 24-hour day. No, the Days of Allah, the Days of Resurrection, the Days of the Son of Man means years, not the common 24-hour day.

What will make us know when we are living in the Days of Allah? It is by the fulfilling of the predictions made by the Prophets of Allah, long before they come to pass. I quote Maulvi Muhammad Ali's footnote 2275 on this verse, in which he says: "The Days of Allah are the contests in which the righteous shall be made successful." That no one can deny for this is a sign for the disbelievers who have enjoyed great temporary prosperity and who thought that they were too rich and powerful to be brought into a state of helplessness. Although they had the histories of those who were before them, there is no difference between the disbeliever's today or the past.

We are living in the Days of Allah. The earth and its people have been ruled by the evil race known as the white race. In these days of Allah, the righteous (the Muslims) are now gaining power over the wicked and will soon rule the earth again as they did before the creation of the white race.

Take notice of my followers who have given up the wicked ways of the white race and their self-styled Christianity and have accepted the Truth. They are gradually becoming the most successful people in the world. Allah has chosen us; we have chosen Allah.

Who can successfully oppose Allah in His Days and time of rule? It is easy for a weak and poverty-stricken people to give up, but it is not so easy when they are powerful and wealthy. They think there will be no end to their power and wealth which is made to deceive them. ***(MTBM pgs. 22-23)***

Holy Qur-an 2:8-9

Deceive only themselves

> 2:8 *And there are some people who say We believe in Allah and the last day and they are not believers.*
>
> 2:9 *They seek to deceive Allah and those who believe, and they deceive only themselves and they perceive not.*

On Hypocrites

A hypocrite, regardless to where he appears or regardless to what organization he may be a member of whether a governmental hypocrite, an industrial hypocrite, a business hypocrite or a religious hypocrite is the most unwanted and hated of all the people concerned. They are also the most hated by God. They are double-crossers; they come in claiming belief and then go out disbelieving.

I quote several passages of the Holy Qur-an on hypocrites of which the average leader or searcher of the scripture has not known, because the scripture teachers here in America have never studied the Holy Qur-an. If they had, they would not be hard to awaken or be united with their own kind.

“Those who disbelieve -- it being alike to them whether thou warn them or warn them not -- they will not believe" (Holy Qur-an 2:6). Allah has sealed their hearts and their hearing; and there is a covering on their eyes, and for them is a grievous chastisement (Holy Qur-an 2:7).

This is not for people who have not known the truth of Allah and His true religion, it is for those who have known and then disbelieve after their believing. The 8th verse of the same chapter reads like this: "And there are some people who say: We believe in Allah and the Last Day, and they are not believers." Verse 9: "They seek to deceive Allah and those who believe, and they deceive only themselves and they perceive not." Verse 10: "In their hearts is a disease, so Allah increased their disease, and for them is a painful chastisement because they lie." Verse 11: "And when it is said to them, Make not mischief in the land, they say: We are but peacemakers." Verse 12: "Now surely they are the mischief makers, but they perceive not." Verse 14: "And when they meet those who believe, they say: We believe; and when they are alone with their devils, they say: Surely we are with you, we were only mocking." Verse 15: "Allah will pay them back their mockery, and He leaves them alone in their inordinacy, blindly wandering on."

In Section 16, entitled "Hypocrites are Dishonest," the Muslims are warned not to try to defend them or contend on behalf of those who act unfaithfully to their souls. "Surely Allah loves not him who is treacherous, sinful." (4:107) "Behold! You are they who may contend on their behalf in this world's life, but who will contend with Allah on their behalf on the Resurrection Day, or who will have charge of their affairs!" (Holy Qur-an 4:109).

In Section 17, entitled "Secret Counsels of the Hypocrites:" "And were it not for Allah's grace upon thee and his mercy, a party of them had certainly designed to ruin thee. And they ruin only themselves, and they cannot harm thee in any way. And Allah has revealed to thee the Book and the Wisdom and taught thee what thou knowest not, and Allah's grace on thee is very great" (Holy Qur-an 4:113).

"There is no good in most of their secret counsels except (in) him who enjoins charity or goodness or reconciliation between people. And whoever does this, seeking Allah's pleasure, We shall give him a mighty reward" (Holy Qur-an 4:114). "And whoever acts hostilely to the Messenger after guidance has become manifest to him and follows other than the way of the believers, We turn him to that to which he (himself) turns and make him enter hell; and it is an evil resort" (Holy Qur-an 4:115).

I have followers who are now fulfilling these verses of the Holy Qur-an; they are true and they are very easy to understand. Allah warns them that He will not aid them against His Messenger but will let them be manifest and bring to a naught their evil plans to destroy the Messenger and the truth which he preaches and even to take his very life and those who are with him.

"And thus have we made in every town the reader of its guilty ones, that they may make plans therein. And they plan not but against themselves and they perceive not" (Holy Qur-an 6:124).

Allah allows the wicked and the leaders of opposition to the Messenger to make their plans therein. And they plan not but against themselves and they perceive not.

Allah allows the wicked and the leaders of opposition to the Messenger to make their plans and try to carry them out against the Messenger. And then Allah makes them to about-face, and the planners of the evil receive the evil results that they wished for the Messenger. (Holy Qur-an 8:46).

"O, Prophet, strive hard against the disbelievers and the hypocrites and be firm against them. And their abode is hell, and evil is the destination," (Holy Qur-an 9:73; read 9:74).

I do not beg anyone to believe, because it is not allowed by Allah for a Messenger to beg people to believe in Allah and His word of truth, neither to take him for an angel or for a Prophet. This is absolutely immaterial on a Prophet's part.

They seek to judge the Messenger of God and (as the Bible teaches) they seek to bring him into courts of the infidels to be judged by them while the Bible and the Holy Qur-an warn you against trying to be the judge of a Messenger of God, in these words: Who is he that judges another man's servant?

The Holy Qur-an repeatedly warns the disbelievers and hypocrites that Allah is sufficient as a judge of His Messenger, and by no means will He let those who molest and seek to destroy His Messenger with their tongues and their hands for no good reason.

There is no excuse for their deviation, only that they were actually hypocrites, eating and feasting with us (as the Bible says), and we did not know they were such people. Allah makes them know whenever he pleases, and I warn you who read this article that these are the days of Judgment, and I am your little brother missioned by God to try to save you from going to the doom of the devil and disbelievers.

Allah is a friend, and I am a friend that He has caused to rise among you, the poor black people of America who have suffered every injustice that man could suffer and are still suffering today.

The enemy cannot be but a hypocrite who will now try to change to offer you friendship. The same enemy who fought and killed you yesterday cannot turn overnight and become your friend.

Be warned and be careful of how you deviate and follow such evil- tongued people as you see now appearing, for in a few days,

God will destroy them all with those whom destruction and justice is due.

May Allah pour upon the hypocrites the chastisement that He poured upon my Mother's son, my own brother who rose up against me in 1935 and joined himself with those who were bent upon taking life away. This was for no cause other than jealousy and envy of my mission. May Allah strike them with terror and grief that they may not have rest day or night for they return to me evil for good. I have been better to them than they were to themselves. Let Allah judge between me and the hypocrites and disbelievers who take Allah and His Messenger and religion for mockery. *(MTBM pgs. 255-258)*

Holy Qur-an 37:65

Devil called serpent

37:65 *Its produce is as it were the heads of serpents.*

God and His Prophets could not have given the white race a better name (serpent) according to the characteristics of that race. The serpent of Genesis 3:1 was none other than the devil (white race). He deceived Adam and his wife, causing them to disobey Allah (God), which was the plan of the serpent (devil), according to the history of the devils. Their greatest desire is to make the righteous disobey the law of righteousness.

They are referred to by this name serpent in the Holy Qur-an (37:65) translated by Maulvi Muhammad Ali: To a tree that grows in the bottom of hell, its produce is as the heads of serpents which the disbelievers shall eat from. In his footnote (2112), he says: That the Arabs apply the name Shaitan to a sort of serpent half a man, ugly or foul in the head and face. In Mr. Abdullah Yusuf Ali's translation of the Holy Qur-an in English, in the same chapter and verse (37:65), it reads: The shoots of its fruit stalks are like the heads of devils. *(MTBM pg. 126)*

Holy Qur-an 7:17

Devil came upon them from before them

> 7:17 *Then I shall certainly come upon them from before them and from behind them, and from their right and from their left, and Thou wilt not find most of them thankful.*

Muhammad set the devils back for 1000 years. They were released on the coming of Columbus, and his finding of this Western Hemisphere. They have been here now over 400 years. Their worst and most unpardonable sins were the bringing of the so-called Negroes here to do their labor.

The so-called Negroes have not only given free labor but have given their lives on the soil of their masters and, all over the earth wherever his hateful and murdering slave-master wants them to go. Now, the slave wants better treatment. They are the children of those who made merchandise out of their fathers. The devil is the "devil" regardless of place and time.

They deceived our fathers are now deceiving the children, under many false disguises, (as though they want to be friends of the black man) such as integration and intermarriage.

The devil said to Allah: "I shall certainly come upon them from behind them; and from their right and from their left; and Thou wilt not find most of them thankful" (Holy Qur-an 7:17). This is being fulfilled before our very eyes today. The devils are doing both.

They come to the so-called Negroes as friends as open enemies. They go before them, changing the truth into false, and come behind the truth-bearer to the so-called Negroes, speaking evil of the truth. They threaten the so-called Negroes with poverty and imprisonment and make rosy promises to them, only to deceive. ***(MTBM pg. 104)***

Holy Qur-an 25:29

Devil deserts man

> 25:29 *Certainly he led me astray from the Reminder after it had come to me. And the devil ever deserts man.*

REGRETS OF THE DOUBTORS

> *"And on the day when the wrongdoer will bite his hands, saying, would that I had taken away with the Messenger!" (Holy Qur-an 25-27)*

According to the histories of the prophets of the past, all of their rejected enemies and mockers of the people had this same regret when the truth of the message that these prophets delivered was made manifest.

And the disbelievers hated themselves for rejecting those warners and prophets of old. The people of Noah showed regret when they saw the flood coming upon them. The people of Sodom and Gomorrah regretted their ignorant acts of disbelieving the truth of Abraham and Lot wished that they had followed Lot out of the city and that they had believed before the fire came so that their cities and their lives would not have been destroyed.

It was also the regret of Pharaoh and his people for not believing the warning that Moses brought to them from Allah. When these rejecters of the Prophets saw their doom approaching, they said, as the disbelievers said in the twenty-seventh verse, that they wished they had followed the prophet.

And so it will be, according to the Bible and Qur-an, with those whom this particular twenty-fifth chapter refers to who reject the last one in the time we are now living in (the resurrection and the judgment). Those of my people and the weak Orthodox Muslims who reject the plain truth and warning that Allah has revealed to me and that I am teaching (to fly to Allah and his true religion of entire submission and submit to His will), do so because of their love for the enemies of Allah, His Prophets and His religion, Islam. They reject this truth to me, the bearer of this truth.

They love the wealth and riches of this people who love not God, the giver of the wealth and riches that they have been so abundantly blessed with. They wish to remain and enjoy the wealth with these people as well as with intermarriage and their sport and play.

They will say what the formal rejecters said, when they see the chastisement of Allah coming upon them and all of their wickedness, evilness and murder. The so-called Negroes of America will also wish they had followed me to Allah.

The biting of their hands, as mentioned in this verse, shows intense grief for their mistake of accepting the false friendship of this evil and murderous race. The white American citizens and the Negroes who are today preaching friendship and intermarriage with their 400-year-old enemies will say these same words, "O woe is me, that I had not taken such a one for a friend" (28th verse).

And they will confess that certainly he leads me astray from the messenger after he had come to me with clear warning and with plain truth (29th verse) and will admit that the devil's promises were all false and he only deceived them in the words given in that same twenty- ninth verse, "And the devil ever deserts man."

What should we set our hearts and minds on today? Finding the right path and walking therein to our God, Allah, and His religion, Islam, that He may make a way for us on some of this earth that we can call our own and deliver us from our open enemies, our deceivers and from evil and filthy doings.

The God of Islam demands us to forsake our enemies and their names and religion and all that goes with them and to completely submit to Him. He, Allah has said to me that He will set us in heaven at once.

Allah's promise is ever true. He fails not in His promise, but this race of devils will promise you and will fail to fulfill it, especially if it is a promise of good. I beg you as a brother and sister of mine, fly to Allah. For the days of the resurrection are not coming, they are here now and the dead are rising as it is written. Let us repeat this prayer:

"O Allah, guide me among those whom Thou hast guided aright and preserve me among those whom Thou has preserved and befriended and bless me in whatever Thou does; grant me and deliver me from the evils of what Thou has judged. Surely Thou judgest and none can judge against Thee and He whom Thou befriended is not disgraced." *(MTBM pgs. 294-296)*

Holy Qur-an 2:208

Devil is your open enemy

> 2:208 *O you who believe, enter into complete peace and follow not the footsteps of the devil. Surely, he is your open enemy.*

Here the Muslim is about to begin his prayer. He has cleansed all the exposed parts of his body, washed out his mouth, nose and ears. Standing upright, with his face towards his Holy City (Mecca), which is in the direction of sunrise, he lifts his cleansed hands up beside his head with the thumbs towards the lobes of his ears and declares that: "Allah is the Greatest" (four times), and that: "Nothing deserves to be worshiped but Allah."

What better preparation could have been made for the service of our God? With due respect and great honor, he is turned in the direction of sunrise in which our planet is carrying him at a speed of 1,037 1/3 miles per hour. Physically, he has turned his face in the direction in which he is traveling, and in which he looks forward to the light of day. From the same direction (sunrise) came all the spiritual light the holy prophets, the holy land and the holy cities of the earth.

With his cleansed hands open, with the palms towards the

Holy Land and cities he signifies an open confession of his internal purity and entire submission to the will of Allah (God). Whatever evils he has committed with his hands, by washing them with the water of life he shows for this his heart's repentance for the evils that his hands have committed.

Now as the open cleansed hands show forth a sincere surrender to their Maker without concealing or hiding anything, so it is with the heart that only Allah (God) can see into is clear of the evils and desires forgiveness, for such evils have been washed from the heart, the ears from hearing them, and the eyes are closed to keep out the evil morals, for none can turn away from me the evil morals but Thee.

The above prayer is preferred as the morning prayer, but can be said by the individual any time that he likes. Here the prayer declares that he is strictly a believer in one God Who originated the universe (the Heavens and earth) and not in three, and further declares "that his sacrifice, life, and death are all for Allah (God) and to Him does he submit." He acknowledges his sins and asks protection against them, or rather against a future sin. *(MTBM pgs. 149-150)*

Chapter 4

Holy Qur-an

7:14 Devil respite me

> 7:14 *He said: Respite me till the day when they are raised.*

The Adamic race is still the enemy of Muslims (the black man). Nevertheless, Allah did not deprive the Adamic race right guidance through His prophets, whom they persecuted and killed. The adamic white races history is proof that they are the enemies of God and the righteous for they never did sincerely accept a prophet of God. Can they now claim to be the chosen race of God? Why would God limit their time of rule? Why did God send His prophets to warn them that He was going to destroy them? Holy Qur-an (7:14)" "He said (the devil) respite me until the day when they are raised up." Those that are referred to a being "raised up" refer to the resurrection of the black man into the knowledge of the white race as being the devils, the enemies of Allah (God) and the black nation. ***(MTBM pg. 134)***

Holy Qur-an 7:21

Devil swear to be sincere adviser

> 7:21 *And he swore to them both: Surely I am sincere adviser to you.*

Holy Qur-an 7:30

Took devil for friends

> 7:30 *A party has He guided, and another party-perdition is justly their due. Surely they took the devils for friends instead of Allah, and they think that they are rightly guided.*

The devil swore to them that he was a sincere adviser (7:21). The Holy Qur-an further says: "Surely they took the devils for friends instead of Allah, and they think that they are right guided" (7:30). Not only the so-called Negroes are deceived by this race of devils, but even many of the Asiatic Muslims do not know that the white race are devils.

Some hate me for teaching this manifest truth of that race; but I want my people here (the so-called Negroes) to wake up and escape the fire that Allah has kindled for their enemies. For they really are not to blame and only need awakening.

Some so-called Negroes, who are in love with the devils, do not like me nor hear it being made manifest. We could lose them without ever missing them; for all who are found believing in, and in love with, the devils will be destroyed with the devils. ***(MTBM pg. 105)***

Holy Qur-an 2:36

Devil's time limited

> 2:36 *But the devil made them slip from it and caused them to depart from the state in which they were. And We said: Go forth, some of you are the enemies of others. And there is for you in the earth an abode and a provision for a time.*

The sword of Islam prevented the Adamic race from crossing the border of Europe and Asia to make trouble among the Muslims for 2000 years after they were driven out of the Holy

Land and away from the people, for their mischief making, lying and disturbing the peace of the righteous nation of Islam.

The Holy Qur-an says: "But the devil made them to depart from that (state) in which they were; and we said: "Get forth, some of you being the enemies of others, and there is for you in the earth an abode and provision for a time!" (The time here refers to the limited time of the Adamic race. The time is 6000 years) According to the above verse (2:36), they were driven out because they were the enemies of the people of the Garden, in these words: "Get forth, some of you being the enemies of others." The others cannot refer to any others than the people of the Garden (the Muslims). *(MTBM pg. 133)*

Holy Qur-an 20:102

Devil with blue eyes

> 20:102 *The day when the trumpet is blown; and We shall gather the guilty, blue-eyed, on that day*

Anyone so blind to the reality of God is the servant of the devil, until he or she sees God as a reality. Thousands of years the devil has been blinding man to God's reality, and that is the reason why God had come in person (and He has) to clear us of such ignorance and blindness to the Knowledge of Him.

Therefore, we have the "Coming of Allah (God)." He is referred to as the Son of Man and gotten for a special purpose, which is to return the lost back to their own and to punish and destroy the wicked for their destruction of the righteous, that the righteous may live in peace and do the will of the God of righteousness, free from trouble and interference. Second, He must be a man to deal with a man, and we cannot receive or respect other than man.

Since His work is to destroy the wicked, He must remain hidden from the eyes of the world until the time is ripe (the end), for the two (God and devil) cannot rule together.

The Son of man (Allah) must wait until His time, after the works of the devil. II Thessalonians 2:8-9; Holy Qur-an 7:14-18 and another place in the Holy Qur-an describes them as the people with the blue eyes (Holy Qur-an 20:102)

Third, the reality of God is as clear as the reality of the devil, but we did not know it until His coming to judge the world. For instance, if we take God for something other than a man (not the man devil), we cannot prove it.

If we believe that He is a spirit and not a man, then we can never expect to have any knowledge of Him except by the sense of feel.

We cannot see spirit; therefore the teachings of his coming would be false. The spirit of life is and has been with us all of our lives God is in person among us today. He is a man, He is in His time. God sees, hears, knows, wills, acts and is a person (man.) The devil workings of the devil must come to an end. ***(MTBM pg. 14)***

Holy Qur-an 61:8-9

Dominate other religion

> 61:8 *They desire to put out the light of Allah with their mouths but Allah will perfect his light, though the disbelievers may be averse.*
>
> 61:9 *He it is, Who sent His Messenger with the guidance and the true religion, that He may make it overcome the religions, all of them, though the polytheists may be averse.*

Holy Qur-an 30:30

Religion of Allah, Islam

> 30:30 *So set thy face for religion, being upright, the nature made by Allah in which He has created men. There is no*

altering Allah's creation. That is the right religion- but most people know not

Holy Qur-an 3:18

True religion with Allah

3:18 Surely the (true) religion with Allah is Islam. And those who were given the Book differed only after knowledge had come to them out of envy among themselves. And whoever disbelieves in the messages of Allah Allah indeed is a Quick at reckoning.

Meaning of Islam

Entire submission to the Will of Allah (God), and His prophets is the national religion of the righteous (Holy Qur-an 30:30), which will dominate all other religions (Holy Qur-an 61:8-9). Surely the true religion of Allah (God) is Islam" (Holy Qur-an 3:18). Can we say this of other religions? Does the Bible give us any prophecy that Christianity will finally rule and dominate the whole world? Islam is the religion which the Holy Qur-an teaches. The Holy Qur-an is a book which white Christianity never has and probably never will introduce to the so-called Negroes. They love for you to read the book (Bible) which they have fixed for you and desire that you never be able to understand it (through the original of the Bible was true.) The Jews are charged with tampering with the original scripture (adding to and taking from it). The Christians are charged with poisoning the original scripture, called the Gospel of Jesus.

Islam means salvation to each and every one who believes in it. To the American so-called Negroes, it is the master key which opens wide every door locked against them. The door of universal friendship with the Creator and His Creatures swings wide open to you and the doors of freedom, justice, and equality. All the believers of Islam are the brothers of the others, unlike Christianity, where the white Christians are too proud to make the black people their equal.

Since the American so-called Negroes never were recognized by white Christianity as equal members, they flocked to the Catholic church to join it, running from a garter snake to a rattlesnake. The garter snake runs from them, the rattlesnake swallows them. They know nothing of the true religion (Islam) of God and care very little, because their minds are to be whatever the white race's minds are.

Christianity has no power for the Negroes against their enemies. Islam is a powerful religion. If the so-called Negroes of the South, or America in general, would accept Allah and His religion, Islam, their dreaded fear of the white man's brutality and murder would be over.

Allah will defend the believers of Islam. The believers are united against their enemies. For every Islamic believing so-called Negro in America, there are 100 Muslim brothers on his or her side. This means if the whole 17 million so-called Negroes were believers in Islam, there would be 17 million of their people with them as brothers and sisters.

Allah's (God) finding of the lost members of the black nation is more valuable in His eyes than the whole world of mankind, and even they are very valuable in the eyes of any Asiatic Muslim. The finding of the so-called Negroes by Allah (God) means the end of the present world and the beginning of a new world under the guidance of Allah (God). ***(MTBM pgs. 71-72)***

Holy Qur-an 2:285

Hear and Obey

> *2:285 "The Messenger believes in what has been revealed to him from his Lord, and (so do) the believers. They all believe in Allah and His angels and His Books and Idis messengers. We make no difference between any of His Messengers. And they say : We hear and obey; our Lord, Thy forgiveness (do we crave) and to Thee is the eventual course."*

Can the proud Christian say with truth the same? No, they don't believe in Allah not to mention His prophets and the scriptures of the prophets; but they like to make a difference in the prophets. All the old prophets are condemned as being other than good, but Jesus they go to the extreme in making Him a Son and finally God. Yet they say that they killed Jesus, the Son of God, because He made Himself the Son of God.

The history of this man Jesus has been gravely misunderstood by us, the American so-called Negroes. *(MTBM pg. 98)*

Holy Qur-an 4:109

Hypocrites are warned

> 4:109 *Behold! You are they who may contend on their behalf in this world's life, but who will contend with Allah on their behalf on the Resurrection day, or who will have charge of their affairs?*

Holy Qur-an 4:115

Those against Messenger enters hell

> 4:115 *And whoever acts hostilely to the messenger after guidance has become manifest to him and follows other than the way of the believers. We turn him to that to which he himself turns and make him enter hell, and it is an evil resort.*

THE TEACHINGS OF THE HOLY QUR-AN ON OBEDIENCE

Say: Obey Allah and the Messenger; but if they turn back, Allah Surely loves not the disbelievers' (Holy Qur-an 3:31).

The religion of Islam demands strict obedience to Allah and His Messenger. The world "Islam" means submission "obedience." Obedience to God (Allah) is not accepted if one is disobedient to the Messenger.

"The Messenger believes in what has been revealed to him from his Lord, and (so do) the believers" (Holy Qur-an 2:285).

A true follower of the Messenger believes as the Messenger believes, but a hypocrite pretends he believes but is not at all a believer. There are those who claim they are believers but are sympathizers of the hypocrites; those are the ones who will never say anything one way or the other, fearing that they will show their sympathy for the hypocrite. Such ones are warned in the Holy Qur-an:

"Behold, you are they who may contend on their behalf in this world's life, but who will contend with Allah on their behalf on the resurrection day" (Holy Qur-an 4:109)

There are those who like to dispute and act hostile toward the Messenger of Allah. They are also warned in the same chapter:

"And whoever acts hostilely to the Messenger after guidance

as become manifest to him and follows other than the way of the believers, we turn him to that to which he himself turns and make him enter hell: And it is an evil resort" (Holy Qur-an 4:115)

This refers to those whom the Messenger has guided to Allah on the right path, and who have tasted the blessings of Allah and then turn back to that which they had been brought out of. And here Allah causes them to meet with a worse condition that they left. This is tasted by such ones in this life. Allah does not spare a Messenger's nearest of kin or their wives and children. (See Holy Qur-an 66:1-11).

Allah will chastise Messengers if they disobey Him, but Allah does not allow us to be the judge of His Messengers, nor does He make a second choice in choosing a Messenger for another. Read the histories of the Prophets of God.

"O you who believe, obey Allah and obey His Messenger and make not your deeds vain."

"Surely those who disbelieve and hinder men from Allah's way then die disbelievers, Allah will not forgive them" (Holy Qur-an 47:33, 34).

God is very hard on those who disobey His Messenger. He warns in His Holy Qur-an not to quarrel and dispute or raise our voices above the Messenger's voice. Strict respect and honor is demanded for His Messengers. We should not take them lightly; we may underestimate them without knowledge. *(MTBM pgs. 259-260)*

Holy Qur-an 7:156

Encompasses all things

> 7:156 *And ordain for us good in this world's life and in the hereafter, for surely we turn to Thee. He said: I afflict with my chastisement whom I please and My mercy compasses all things. So I ordain it for those who keep their duty and pay the poor rate, and those who believe in our messages-*

THE PRINCIPLES OF ISLAM

The number one principle of Islam is a belief in Allah (God); the belief in a power higher than man. Although man may be ignorant of just who it is who has such supreme power, it can be traced back to the beginning of the civilization of the human race and to the beginning of the writing of history. Regardless of tribes and national gods, there still exists the belief in a greater God that was more powerful than their national gods or those who were molded by their own hands out of clay, wood, iron, silver, gold and stone. Some of these gods were the leaders of their tribes or people. There were fire gods and birds, animals, snakes, beasts and even trees were worshiped as God.

The God in Islam is not a national or tribal god, but as the Holy Qur-an describes Him in the opening words, "He is the Lord of the Worlds." This conception of God is best, since man's belief is by nature, that there must exist somewhere in the universe one who has and can exercise a great power than can he or the object that he is bowing to as his god. The Islam God is One of Whom there is no equal! One to Whom whatsoever is in the heavens and whatsoever is in the earth submits willingly or unwillingly. He is the Lord of the Creation of the Universe, and since He has no equal, He demands universal recognition and complete submission to His will.

All religions, directly or indirectly, recognize and preach the Oneness of God. The conception of a Divine Supreme Being is accepted by all intelligent human beings—even savages recognize a power that is supreme. Islam rejects the belief in the plurality of persons in the Godhead. Say, "He Allah is one, Allah is He of Whom nothing is independent but upon Whom we all depend. He begets not, nor is He begotten and there is none like Him."

In another place it reads: "And my mercy encompasses all things" (Holy Qur-an 7:156), Muhammad Ali says: "The great Apostle of the Unity of God could not conceive of a god who was not the author of all that existed. Such detraction from His power and knowledge would have given a death blow to the very loftiness and sublimity of the conception of the divine Supreme Being." But, until today, the true knowledge of the One, Divine Supreme Being, is known only to a few. We are daily coming into the knowledge of this One God. There are some people who think that God is something that cannot be seen or felt. A belief in God is the first principle of Islam. ***(MTBM pgs. 72-73)***

Holy Qur-an 2:2

Fear Allah

> 2:2 *This Book, there is no doubt in it, is a guide to those who keep their duty.*

Both books are called holy. The word of Allah (God) is holy, and His word is true. Therefore, all truth is holy, for Allah (God) is holy and is the author of truth, without the shadow of a doubt! Allah is the representative of the Holy Qur-an (not a prophet) in these words: "This book, there is no doubt of it, is a guide to those who guard against evil" (2:2), translated by Maulvi Muhammad

Ali. Abdullah Yusuf Ali's translation of the same verse reads nearly the same: "This is the book; in it is guidance, sure, without doubt to those who fear Allah (God)" (2:2) *(MTBM pg. 86)*

Holy Qur-an 7:18

Fear Allah

> 7:18 *He said: Get out of it, despised driven away. Whoever of them will follow thee, I will certainly fill hell with you all.*

Holy Qur-an 15:43

Fear Allah

> 15:43 *And surely hell is the promised place for them all--*

SUBMIT TO ALLAH (GOD) AND FEAR NOT

Islam, the religion of entire submission to the will of Allah (God). "Nay, whoever submits his whole self to Allah and is a doer of good, he will get his regard with his Lord, on such shall be no fear, nor shall they grieve. " (Holy Qur-an 2:112).

That and that alone is Salvation according to the Holy Qur-an. Fear is a number one enemy that is blocking progress and success from coming to the so-called Negroes of America. This fear causes them to grieve. The whole world knows the poor so-called Negroes of America have suffered and still suffer more grief and sorrow than any people on the earth! This fear is the fear of a slave-masters (white man) and what the slave-masters dislike. Let the so-called Negroes submit to Allah (God) and they will not fear anymore, nor will they grieve. As it is written: "The fear of man bringeth a snare. " (Proverbs:29). It has surely snared the so-called Negroes.

The Lord of the world's Finder of we the lost members of the Asiatic Black Nation for 400 years said that the slave-masters put fear in our Fathers when they were babies. Allah is the only one that can remove this fear from us, but he will not remove it from us until we submit to His will, not our will, and fear Him and Him alone. Then, as it is written, "And it shall come to pass in the day that the Lord shall give thee rest from sorrow and from thy fear, and from the hard bondage wherein thou wast made to serve."(Isaiah 14:3). There are so many places that I could point out in the Bible and Holy Qur-an that warn us of fearing our enemies above or equal to the fear of Allah (God). It is a fool who has greater fear of the devils (white man) than Allah who has the power to destroy the devils and their followers (Revelation 21:8; Holy Qur-an 7:18 and 15:43).

We must remember that if Islam means entire submission to the will of Allah, that and that alone is the True religion of Allah. Do not you and your religious teachers and the Prophets of old teach that the only way to receive God's help or Guidance is to submit to his will! then WHY NOT ISLAM! It (Islam) is the true religion of Allah and the ONLY way to success. ***(MTBM pgs. 29-30)***

Chapter 5

Holy Qur-an 7:18

Fill hell with you all

> 7:18 *He said: Get out of it, despised driven away. Whoever of them will follow thee, I will certainly fill hell with you all.*

After what? May be the question asked. The hereafter means after the destruction of the present world, its power and authority to rule. The Bible and Holy Qur-an Sharrieff are filled with readings on the hereafter which I will leave to you to read for proof. This subject wouldn't be necessary if it were not for that man of sin being permitted to rule.

Since he (they) was given ruling authority to try him [them] for 6000 years, the word "hereafter is used; meaning: after the present rule of the man of sin, because his [their] time is limited to 6000 years. Some say: after the judgment, after the man when the man of sin and all who follow him were made." Whoever of them will follow you, I will certainly fill hell with you all" (Holy Qur-an 7:18). The Bible says: "These both were cast alive into a lake of fire" (Rev. 19:20) The man of sin and his people deceived the righteous by making them believe that he [they] also is one of the righteous. He [they] claims one father is the father of all, but that is not true. ***(MTBM pg. 303)***

Holy Qur-an 7:18

Fill hell with you all

> *7:18 He said: Get out of it, despised driven away. Whoever of them will follow thee, I will certainly fill hell with you all.*

They came to the so-called Negroes as friends as open enemies. They go before them, changing the truth into false; and come behind the truth-bearer to the so-called Negroes, speaking evil of the truth. They threaten the so-called Negroes with poverty and imprisonment, and make rosy promises to them, only to deceive.

They are telling the so-called Negroes that they realized that they used to mistreat the Negroes but now they are going to do better and forget the past. “Let us live like brothers for we are all from God. Along with such smooth lies is an offer of one of the devils’ women. The poor so-called Negroes fall victim and the devil men raid the neighborhood of the so-called Negro women, day & night, to make all desirous of hell fire.

This is the way they have planned to treat Allah to the so-called Negroes what should you do? The answer: Stay away from sweet hearting with devils. Surely this is the end of their time, on our planet. Allah said to the devil: “Get out of it despised, and driven away. Whoever of them (the Negroes) will follow you, I will certainly fill hell with you all.” (7:18) So remember, your seeking friendship with this race of devils means seeking a place in their hell. ***(MTBM pgs. 104-105)***

Holy Qur-an 32:3

Follow right direction

> *32:3 Or do they say: He has forged it? Nay, it is the Truth from thy Lord that thou mayest warn a people to whom no warn has come before thee that they may walk aright.*

What I am trying to make clear is that white people do not believe in Allah and Islam or Prophets of Allah. Why then, should you seek the truth of it from them? You will soon come to know that you should not seek any truth from them. They have you following in the wrong direction and hope to keep you like that; but try my Allah's power and wisdom, and my life's blood, you shall know the truth even against your own will.

They (white people) have nearly all of the poor black preachers on their side to oppose Allah, myself and Islam, the religion of the righteous. They will fail and be brought to disgrace as Pharaoh's magicians & he himself were by Allah (God), for you have not known Him, or His religion, as Israel had not known God by his name Jehovah (Exod. 6:3).

They felt that they should not believe Moses representation of God by any other name than God Almighty, regardless of Moses' stress upon Jehovah as being the God of their fathers. Pharaoh had not used that name (Jehovah). So Israel would not accept it until a showdown between Jehovah and Pharaoh. I would not like to have you wait until a showdown between Allah and the modern Pharaoh's people; therefore I come to you with the truth, verifying that which is before it, and giving good news to the believers that they most certainly shall have heaven in this life. I also come to you with a warning to those who disbelieve that you most certainly shall have hell in this life, and the hereafter you most certainly will be among the losers, or do they say, "He has forged it?" Nay, it is the truth from the Lord, that you may warn a people to whom no warning has come before, that they may follow the right direction (HQ 32-3). ***(MTBM pgs. 21-22)***

Holy Qur-an 32:1–2

Lord of the Worlds

32:1 *I, Allah, am the Best Knower.*

32:2 *The revelation of the Book, there is no doubt in it, is from the Lord of the worlds.*

Holy Qur-an 32:23

Gave Book to Moses

> 32:33 *And we indeed gave Moses the Book so doubt not the meeting with him and we made it a guide for the children of Israel.*

The Bible does not claim God to be its author. Jehovah calls to Moses out of the burning bush to go to Pharaoh (Ex. 3:10). There is no mention of a book on Bible that is found that Jehovah gave to Moses in the first five books of the Bible, which are claimed to be Moses' books. Moses' rod is the only thing used against Pharaoh and the land of Egypt, and tablets of stone in the mountains of Sinai. The miraculous rod of Moses, and not a book, brought Pharaoh and his people to their doom. The Ten Commandments served as a guide for the Jews in the Promised Land. Where do we find in the Bible that it was given to Moses by Jehovah under such name as Bible on the Book?

But, on the other hand, Allah (God) tells that He gave the Book, the Holy Qur-an, to Muhammad. "I am Allah, the best Knower, the revelation of the book there is no doubt in it, it is from the Lord of the worlds" (Sura 32:1,2). Allah says to Muhammad in the same above (Sura 32:23): "We gave the book to Moses, and be not in doubt in receiving it, we made it a guide for the children of Israel."

If Moses' rod and book were given as a guide for Israel, and the gospel God gave to Jesus as a guide and warning to the Christians and the Holy Qur-an to Muhammad for the Arab world, will God give us (the so-called Negroes) a book as a guide for us?

If we are in the change of two worlds (Christianity and Islam), then surely, we need a "new book" for our guidance; for those books have served the people to whom they were given. But all on both books are guidance for us all. Yet we must have a new book for the "new change" that which no eye has seen nor ear has heard, nor has entered into our hearts what it is like. We know these books; they have been seen and handled by both good and no good. Certainly the Holy Qur-an is from the Lord of the Worlds, there can be no doubt in the word of Allah (God). But if the book or books have the words of someone else other than Allah's words in it or them, there is no doubt in our hearts concerning the receiving of such book or books. *(MTBM pgs. 86-87)*

Holy Qur-an 4:163 & 165

Givers of good news and as warners

> 4:163 *Surely we have revealed to thee as we revealed to Noah and the prophets after him, and we revealed to Abraham and Ishmael and Isaac and Jacob and the tribes, and Jesus and Job and Jonah and Aaron and Solomon, and we gave to David a scripture.*
>
> 4:165 *Messengers, bearers of good news and warners, so that the people may have no plea against Allah after the (coming of) messengers. And Allah is even Mighty, Wise.*

Holy Qur-an 16:36

Shun the devil

> 16:36 *And certainly, we raised in every nation a messenger saying: Serve Allah and shun the devil. Then of them was he whom Allah guided, and of them was he whose remaining in error was justly due. So, travel in the land, then see what was the end of the rejectors.*

They were offered Islam by Musa (Moses), Jesus, Muhammad and many other prophets, but they rejected it. "And certainly, we raised in every nation an apostle saying serve Allah and shun the devils. So, there were others against whom error was due; therefore, travel in the land, then see what was the end of the rejectors." (Holy Qur-an 16:36)

The prophets had delivered to them the message of truth and shown them the right way; but they chose to remain in error (evil doings). This stands true of this people today. They know the truth, and right from wrong but they like wrong or evil better than right; therefore, they are against Islam and its truth. The Holy Qur-an says:

"Surely, we have revealed to you as we revealed to Noah and the Prophets after him, and we revealed to Abraham and Ishmael and the tribes, and Jesus, Job and Jonah, Aaron, Solomon and we gave to David a scripture. We sent apostles as the givers of good news and as warners, so that people should not have a plea against Allah after the coming of the Apostles." (4:136, 165). The Messengers of Allah (God) bring good news to the people, but if that good news is rejected, therefore they are warned that bad news will come.

The Christian white world, whose leader and teacher is the Pope of Rome (The Father of the Church) claims that Jesus brought a new religion to them. But the scripture of both Bible and Holy Qur-an denies such false charge and makes Jesus' religion the same as the Prophets' who were before Him. Muhammad was also given the same religion of Jesus and the Prophets before Him. ***(MTBM pgs. 131-132)***

Holy Qur-an 30:17

Glorify Allah

> 30:17 *So glory be to Allah when you enter the evening and when you enter the morning.*

Holy Qur-an 2:284

He forgives whom he pleases

> 2:284 *To Allah belongs whatever is in the heavens and whatever is in the earth. And whether you manifest what is in your minds or hide it, Allah will call you to account according to it. So He forgives whom He pleases and chastises whom He pleases. And Allah is Possessor of power over all things.*

Holy Qur-an 61:9

He it is who sent His Apostle

> [61:9] *He it is who sent His Messenger with the guidance and the true religion, that he may make it overcome the religions--all of them, though the polytheists may be averse.*
>
> *"He it is who sent His Apostle with the guidance and the true religion, that He may make it overcome the religions, all of them, though the polytheists may be averse." According to the Holy Qur-an 61:9*

In the above verse Allah (God) in the last days of this present world (wicked and infidel) states that he must destroy false religions with the true religion (Islam). It (Islam) must overcome all other religions. The verse also teaches us that Allah in the judgment of the world will not recognize any religion other than Islam.

Take to task all the learned teachers of religions, and they will admit that God is One and that He will have only one religion in the hereafter.

Search the scriptures of the Bible and Holy Qur-an and be convinced. There are two other religions today that oppose the religion of peace (Islam) namely Buddhism and Christianity. These two opposing forces will be removed from the people completely by the light of Islam, Truth, guided by Allah in the person of the Great Mahdi, Fard Muhammad. I am His Apostle. It will come to pass that you will not even find a trace of them. Christianity is already dying a natural death. We want a religion of peace, freedom, justice and equality. We want it from the Divine Supreme Being Allah and not a religion prepared by the hand of His (Allah's) enemies. *(MTBM pg. 76)*

Holy Qur-an 63:1-3

Hypocrites are Liars

63:1 When the hypocrites come to thee, they say: We bear witness that thou art indeed His Messenger. And Allah Knows thou art indeed His Messenger. And Allah bears witness that the hypocrites are surely liars.

63:2 They take shelter under their oaths, thus turning (men) from Allah's way. Surely, evil is that which they do.

63:3 That is because they believed then disbelieved; thus, their hearts are sealed, so they understand not.

Holy Qur-an 4:150-151

Hypocrites Warned against trying to deceive

Holy Qur-an 4:152

Reward for those believers in Allah and His Messenger

4:150 Those who disbelieve in Allah and His messengers and desire to make a distinction between Allah and His Messengers and say: We believe in some and disbelieve in others; and desire to take a course in between-

4:151 These are truly disbelievers; and we have prepared for the disbelievers an abrasing chastisement.

4:152 And those who believe in Allah and His messengers and make no distinction between any of them, to them He will grant their rewards. And Allah is ever Forgiving, Merciful.

They desire to make the Messenger think that they are true believers by saying that they believe that he is the Messenger of Allah, while in their hearts they do not believe that he is the Messenger and Allah Knows what is in their hearts that they are liars. They come in believing & then disbelieve. After their disbelieved Allah seals their hearts so that they cannot understand or believe. In the 150th verse of the 4th Chapter: they are warned against trying to deceive Allah and His Messenger. They say that they believe in one and disbelieve in the other. But disbelief in God or His Apostle means a disbelief in both.

This Verse (4:150) reads like this: Those who disbelieve in Allah and His messengers and desire to make a distinction between Allah and His Messengers and say: We believe in some and disbelieve in others; and desire to take a course in between [4:151]. These are truly disbelievers; and we have prepared for the disbelievers an abrasing chastisement."

Holy Qur-an [4:152] reads: "And those who believe in Allah and His messengers and make no distinction between any of them, to them He will grant their rewards. And Allah is ever Forgiving, Merciful."

This is going on today among my followers. Many of the hypocrites who go out from me will still say to you that they believe in Allah but do not believe that I am the Messenger of Allah. This is as if they said that they do not believe in either one of us. You cannot get to Allah unless you come through his Messenger, Apostle or Prophet of Allah. When a hypocrite begins disbelieving, the light is taken from him, and he is not able to see that he is actually a disbeliever. It is like someone wandering around in darkness but claiming that he sees his way while the person in the light, looking on the dark, knows that he is not able to see his way around. ***(MTBM pgs. 252-253)***

Holy Qur-an 5:53

Hypocrites seek friends with enemy of Islam

5:53 And those who believe will say: Are these they who swore by Allah with their most forcible oaths that they were surely with you? Their deeds will bear no fruit, so they will be losers.

Holy Qur-an 4:144-145

No help for hypocrite

4:44 O you who believe take not the disbelievers for friends rather than the believers. Do you desire to give Allah a manifest proof against yourselves?

4:145 The hypocrites are surely in the lowest depths of the Fire, and thou wilt find no helper for them,

Holy Qur-an 47:23, 25-28

Hypocrites practice deceit

47:23 Those it is whom Allah has cursed, so He has made them deaf and blinded their eyes.

47:25 Surely those who turn back after guidance is manifest to them, the devil embellishes it for them; and lengthens false hopes for them.

47:26 That is because they say to those who hate what Allah has revealed: We will obey you in same matters. And Allah Knows their secrets.

47:27 But how will it be when the angels cause them to die, smiting their faces and their backs?

47:28 That is because they follow that which displeases Allah and are averse to His pleasure, so He makes their deeds fruitless.

Holy Qur-an 66:9-10

Messenger warned not to be easy on hypocrites.

66:9 O Prophet, strive against the disbelievers and the hypocrites, and remain firm against them, and their abode is hell; and evil is the resort.

66:10 Allah sets faith in example for those who disbelieve the wife of Noah and the wife of Lot. They were both under two of Our righteous servants, but they acted treacherously towards them, so they availed them naught against Allah, and it was said: Enter the fire with those who enter.

The Prophet is warned to strive hard against the hypocrites and disbelievers and be unyielding to them, for their abode is the "Fire of Hell." The relation between the hypocrites and the believers is cut off. They are not allowed to go around the Muslims. Not even charity is accepted from hypocrites by the believers. They seek friendship with the enemies of Islam. Read Chapter 5, Verse 53 (Holy Qur-an), and also Chapter 4 verses 144 and 145. There is no help for the hypocrites. They practice deceit. Read Chapter 47, Verse 23, and also verses 25 through 28.

This particular group (hypocrites) should always be watched by the believers. They are very deceitful and must be opposed by all means. They are not to be killed, for Allah desires to make them examples for others by chastising them like a parent does a child. He chastises one with the strap to warn the other not to disobey. After a divine chastisement of the hypocrites, they are turned into the doom of the real enemies (the devils). That is why the Holy Qur-an speaks of them as inmates of the "Fire of Hell."

The Messenger is warned not to be easy with hypocrites but to be hard against them. Read Chapter 66, Verse 10, as well as Chapter 66, Verse 9, which even warns the Messenger that there were prophets who had hypocritical wives. This makes it clear to us that not only the common people can have a hypocrite in the family, but also the families of prophets.

Because of this, some people will think you are weak. They will say: "Oh, if his wife does not believe in him, he must not be the Messenger of God." If his sons and daughters do not believe in him, they say: "They should know more about him than we do. He must not be the Messenger."

But this does not mean that the Messenger is not the true one. Jesus prophesied that the truth will cause separation in the family. Mothers and fathers believing with children disbelieving.

And children believing with mothers and fathers disbelieving.

This is going on now. There are many who come to us saying that they believe and want to join with us who believe in Allah and His truth and His Messenger, but many times their parent and/or children do not believe. This is the Judgment Day which you have been warned will come. The truth of Almighty God that I preach to you is not denied by scholars or scientists who understand. And if they do not understand, send them to me, and when they leave me, they will understand that it is the truth.

Chapter 104 of the Holy Qur-an is entitled the Slanderer. Please read it and the footnote (#2794), which fits very well with the slander I am now receiving from the chief hypocrites. ***(MTBM pgs. 253-254)***

Chapter 6

Holy Qur-an 7:16

I will lie in wait

> *7:16 He said: As Thou hast adjudged me to be erring, I will certainly lie in wait for them in Thy straight path,*

He as (the devil) said: Thou hast caused me to remain disappointed, I will certainly lie in wait for them in Thy straight path" (Holy Qur-an 7:16). What Allah disappointed the devils in was the limiting of their rule over the actions and making it manifest to the world of black man that they are the enemies and great deceivers of the righteous.

The white race is not, and never will be the chosen people of Allah (God). They are the chosen people of their father Yakub, the devil. ***(MTBM pg. 134)***

Holy Qur-an 1:1-7

In The Name of Allah

In the name of Allah the Beneficent, the Merciful.

> *1:1 Praise be due to Allah, the Lord of the worlds,*
>
> *1:2 The Beneficent the Merciful,*
>
> *1:3 Master of the day of Requital.*
>
> *1:4 Thee do we serve and Thee do we beseech for help.*
>
> *1:5 Guide us on the right path,*

1:6 The path of those upon whom Thou hast bestowed favors,

1:7 Not of those upon whom wrath is brought down, nor of those who go astray.

What a good prayer for one who is lost from the right direction as the so-called Negroes are to pray. They (the white race) cannot regain paradise because they are not members of that family. But, on the other hand, the lost-found so -called Negroes are really, by nature, members of the original family of paradise. It was by prayer and the turning in the right direction (toward the Holy Temple Mecca) that delivered Jonah from the belly of the fish (Jonah 2:2-4) which is only a type of us here in America (the anti-typical fish) who has swallowed us.

Our prayers will be speedily heard, and Allah will fight our battles against our enemies and bring them to disgrace. ***(MTBM pg.141)***

Holy Qur-an 2:40-41

Keep your duty to Me

2:40 O Children of Israel, call to mind My favor which I bestowed on you and be faithful to (your) covenant with Me, I shall fulfil (My) covenant with you; and Me, Me alone, should you fear.

2:41 And believe in that which I have revealed, verifying that which is with you, and be not the first to deny it; neither take a mean price for My messages; and keep your duty to Me, Me alone.

Holy Qur-an 2:42

Mix Not Up The Truth

2:42 And mix not up truth with falsehood, nor hide the truth while you know.

THE TRUTH

The Holy Qur-an is a great book when it is understood. The above verse warns against mixing Truth with falsehood, as it is the policy of the devils. But nearly all the religious leaders of Christianity are guilty of mixing up the Divine Truth with falsehood. Now they don't know which is Truth and which is falsehood. They are really confused, thinking and planning against the Truth, trying to hide falsehood. They mixed up the Truth of the Bible so much that today they admit someone has tampered with the book. The Bible now teaches against evil and for evil. For instance, it says that we should not drink strong drinks; wine is prohibited in some places and in others it says that it is good for us.

The Truth must triumph over falsehood, as day triumphs over night. When we deny the truth it shows that we love falsehood more than truth. If we fear to speak the truth for the sake of falsehood, this is not only hiding the truth, but is actually showing fear and distrust in the Divine Supreme Being, His wisdom and His power.

This hiding and mixing the truth with falsehood because of fear of the enemy (devils) is taking a great number of our people to hell with the devils.

It is natural for one to fear that of which he has no knowledge. However, when Truth and Knowledge are made clear to you, you have no cloak for your fear.

Your mixing up Truth with falsehood is only because you fear your enemy (the devils).

Allah (God) doesn't care for us when our fear is greater for our enemies than for Him. Allah says: I and I alone, should you fear. Believe in that which I have revealed, verifying that which is with you, and be not the first to deny it; neither take a mean price for my message; and keep your duty to Me, and to Me alone (Holy Qur-an 2:40-41).

Once the so-called Negroes drop slavery (Christianity), and accept Allah for their God, and His religion (Islam) Allah will remove their fear and grief, and they will not fear nor grieve any more.

It is a shame to see our people in such a fearful condition. The fearful and the unbelieving shall have their part in the lake which burns with fire and brimstone which is the second death" (Rev. 21:8).

The devil whom they fear more than Allah (God) was not able to protect himself against Allah; therefore his followers shared with him the fire of hell. They had suffered one death (mental), and by fearing the devils and rejecting the truth, they suffered a physical death, which was the final death.

The devils know that they have deceived the world with their false religion (Christianity). The devils are so afraid that Islam is going to give life and light to the so-called Negroes that they sit and watch over them day and night. ***(MTBM pgs. 98-99)***

Holy Qur-an 7:26-27

Let not the devil seduce you

> 7:26 *O children of Adam, We have indeed sent down to you clothing to cover your shame, and (clothing) for beauty; and clothing that guards against evil—that is the best. This is of the messages of Allah that they may be mindful.*
>
> 7:27 *O children of Adam, let not the devil seduce you, as he expelled your parents from the garden, pulling off from them their clothing that he might show them their shame. He surely sees you, he as well as his host, from whence you see them not. Surely We have made the devils to be the friends of those who believe not.*

You are letting the devils fool and disgrace you and are taking you to hell with them! Your God, Allah, will be happy and will rejoice in feeding, clothing and sheltering you if you believe. The Bible teaches you that He fed and sheltered Israel in the desert

(Exod. 16:12-15). Fear not, Allah (God) is with us. The enemies of Allah and the righteous are leading you only to evil and indecency, as the Holy Qur-an teaches you and me.

They are pulling off your clothes and showing the world your shame, and you think it is right. They are used to going nude. They have nudist colonies here in America to prove it. Four thousand years ago all of Europe was a nudist colony. And your little daughters are being brought up to not be shy of indecency.

You have them stripped to their trunks, all because the devils invited you to wear such styles of theirs, and you are obeying. This is to tempt the black people in becoming sharers in their doom.

Your common sense teaches you that God does not approve of such filth. This should also bring you into the knowledge that the religion (Christianity) so talked and preached of by the white race is only a bit for you to swallow to become the followers of them (the enemies of God). Your loving and sweet-hearting them only means that you are in love with the devils in person, and you are courting death and hell fire. Believe this or leave it. Read Holy Qur-an 7:27, O children of Adam, let not the devil seduce you, as he expelled your parents from the garden (this was done by the father of this race, Yakub, 6,000 years ago) pulling off from their clothing that he might show them their shame, he surely sees you as his host.

They make fools of you and then laugh at you for being dumb enough for them to trick. (The devil scientists and rulers prepare the trap for you and the others spring it on you.) The above verse you are now fulfilling by going partly nude. You have confidence in the devils because you do not know them to be devils. You are now being taught, and there will be no excuse for your taking them for friends instead of Allah.

The clothing that guards against evil is the knowledge of good and evil, the reward of good and the consequences of doing evil and the good of both. Again, the above verses (26, 27) answer the lie (that you are not able to feed and clothe your children and that you should not have many children) that the devils are tricking you into birth control in order to sterilize the so-called Negroes of America.

Beware, my dear sister, the tricks of your enemies and mine, the devils. *(MTBM pgs 101-102)*

Holy Qur-an 10:104

My religion

> *10:104 Say: O people, if you are in doubt as to my religion, then (know that) I serve not those whom you serve besides Allah, but I serve Allah, Who causes you to die; and I am commanded to be of the believers,*

ISLAM FOR SO-CALLED NEGROES

> *Say: "O people, if you are in doubt as to my religion, [Islam] then know that I do not serve those whom you serve besides Allah, Who will cause you to die." (Holy Qur-an 10:104)*

According to the past histories of prophets and reformers, the very people to whom they were sent with the light of truth were their rejecters and even their enemies. When the time comes for a change in the life of a people, there are those who will not appreciate a change. They are suspicious and doubt that which is other than what they have been believing all their lives. The people of Noah, Abraham, Moses and Jesus doubted that which these prophets brought to them from Allah (God) until Allah brought about a showdown between the two.

The so-called American Negroes have been so gravely deceived by the white man's Christianity and Bible that they doubt everything that does not have the white man's approval. Again, the time has arrived for a change. This time is universal, and the great problem now is to awaken the American so-called Negroes.

The so-called Negroes are made to believe that all religions other than the Christian religion are false and idol worship. While the Christians worship idol gods in their churches and religious literature. They bow in reverence to statues and imaginary pictures of God, the angels, the prophets and the disciples as if they could speak. Worst of all, the pictures and statues are not of God, His angels, the Prophets, or the disciples of Jesus. Therefore, they are false worshipers and ignorant enough to love the falsehood. Isaiah and Ezekiel have well described them. The Christian believers claim to believe in One God. Should not the Divine Supreme Being destroy those who serve and worship gods other than He? Allah (God) does not approve of you and me worshiping His angels and prophets as His equal. It is a disgrace.

The religion of Islam teaches that Allah is One God, and the Holy Qur-an teaches that what you worship besides Allah is the firewood of hell. You doubt the Truth of Islam, while it is the religion of Allah (God) and the prophets whom you claim to believe in.

Again, the principles of belief in Islam are: One God, his Prophets, His Scriptures, His Judgment, His Resurrection (of the mentally dead). The main principles of action in Islam: keeping up prayer, spending in the cause of truth, fasting especially during the month of Ramadan, pilgrimage to Mecca, speaking the truth regardless of to whom or what, being clean internally, loving your brother believers as yourself, doing good to all, killing no one whom Allah has ordered not to be killed, setting at liberty the captured believer, worshiping no god but Allah, and fearing no one but Allah. These are the teachings of the prophets. ***(MTBM pgs. 81-82)***

Holy Qur-an 2:112

No fear for Him

2:112 *Nay, whoever submits himself entirely to Allah and he is the doer of good (to others), he has his reward from his Lord, and there is no fear for such nor shall they grieve.*

It (Islam) is the only religion that gives the believer a peace— of mind and contentment. It removes grief and fear at once on believing. *(MTBM pg. 70)*

Holy Qur-an 40:4

None dispute Message but those who disbelieve

40:4 None dispute concerning the messages of Allah but those who disbelieve, so let not their control in the land deceive thee.

The preceding verse is very clear. According to the Holy Qur-an , the truth must always be rejected—and classified as foolishness by the rejectors. It is always those who consider themselves to be in the seat of authority and power in the land who reject the truth. They desire to lead others in their rejection of the truth, especially the poor man in the mud, because he is the one whom they exploit.

Their rejective behavior is similar to that of the people in the land of America today. The white man is in control, and he seeks to deceive the so-called Negro just as Pharaoh deceived the Israelites. Pharaoh had control and power over Egypt. He made a mockery of Moses saying that Moses could not speak plainly, and he criticized Allah's offer to Israel. Pharaoh did not give the Israelites that promised land of milk and honey (fertility and riches).

The white man in America is like Pharaoh in Egypt. He, the modern Pharaoh, is trying to control the 22 million so-called American Negroes as Pharaoh did the Israelites in Egypt. The white man's control over the so-called Negro makes them helpless in trying to follow Allah and His servant into a land they call their own and where they can rule themselves as other nations are doing.

The so-called Negroes are deceived in thinking their future in America will be a great one. They should accept their own (Islam) and—try to do something for themselves as other nations are doing, on land they can call their own. They have intelligence but do not have the desire to do for themselves. Consequently, the white man of America is helping them to continue to have such foolish desires. He wants to keep the so-called Negro looking up to the white American for what he wants. *(MTBM pgs. 206-207)*

Holy Qur-an 4:163

None other than Islam

4:13 Surely We have revealed to thee as We revealed to Noah and the prophets after him, and We revealed to Abraham and Ishmael and Isaac and Jacob and the tribes, and Jesus and Job and Jonah and Aaron and Solomon, and We gave to David a scripture.

The dominant religion of the East is Islam. The holy religious teachings of all the prophets from Adam to Muhammad, was none other than Islam (Holy Qur-an 4:163). They all were of the East and came from that direction with the light of the Truth and shone towards the old wicked darkness of the West. But the West has ever closed its eyes and thus making it necessary for the coming of the Son of Man, the Great Mahdi, God in person.

Being the end of the signs, in His person, He dispels falsehood with the truth as the sun dispels night on its rising from the East. Why should the tribes of the earth mourn because of the coming of the Son of Man, instead of rejoicing? *(MTBM pg. 13)*

Holy Qur-an 2:62

Nor shall they grieve

2:62 Surely those who believe, and those who are Jews, and the Christians and the Sabians, whoever believes in Allah and the Last Day and does good, they have their reward with their Lord, and there is no fear for them, nor shall they grieve.

The religion of Islam is everything that we need for salvation. The poor black man is waking up to this truth and is coming into Islam by the thousands, against the wishes of the whites, because of the love and unity & universal friendship which Islam brings to the believers. This is what the poor black man of America needs more of —TRUE FRIENDS! He gets them in Islam! The white race has and still is trying to keep us from having true friends among our own kind or even among ourselves here in America. Because of the truth of Islam, they are now charging that is fans hate against them. ***(MTBM pg. 132)***

Chapter 7

Holy Qur-an 49:13

Holy Qur-an 76:2

O 'mankind, surely we created you.

> 49:13 *O mankind, surely we have created you from a male and a female, and made you tribes and families that you may know each other. Surely the noblest of you with Allah is the most dutiful of you. Surely Allah is Knowing, Aware.*
>
> 76:2 *Surely We have created man from sperm mixed (with ovum), to try him, so We have made him hearing, seeing.*

Again, we learn who the Bible (Genesis 1:26) is referring to in the saying: "Let us make man."

This "US" was fifty-nine thousand nine hundred and ninety-nine (59, 999) black men and women; making or grafting them into the likeness or image of the original man.

Now that they are the same, but have the ways of a human being they are referred to as "mankind" —not the real original man, but a being made like the original in the sense of human beings.

The Holy Qur-an throws a great light on the truth of the creating of this pale, white race of devils.

"O mankind, surely we have created you from a male and a female" (Chapter 49:13). This makes it very easy to understand to whom it is referring. "What mankind?" Surely we created man from sperm mixed (with ovum) to try him, so we have made him hearing and seeing" (Chap 76:2).

In as much as these chapters have as further reference to the spiritual creation of the last Messenger, it is equally true that they refer to the physical creation of the white race. In another place, the Holy Qur-an says: "We have created man, and now he is an open disputer." ***(MTBM pgs. 118-119)***

Also, Read "Making of the Devil" in Message to the Blackman.

Holy Qur-an 2:30

One who shall rule

> 2:30 *And when thy Lord said to the angels, I am going to place a ruler in the earth, they said: Wilt Thou place in it such as make mischief in it and shed blood? And we celebrate Thy praise and extoll Thy holiness. He said: Surely I know what you Know not.*

According to the word of Allah (God) and the history of the world, since the grafting of the Caucasian race 6000 years ago, they have caused more bloodshed than any people Known to the black nation.

Born murderers, their very nature is to murder. The Bible and Holy Qur-an Sharrieff are full of teachings of this bloody race of devils. They shed the life blood of all, life even their own, and are scientist at deceiving the black people.

They deceived the very people of Paradise (Bible, Gen 3:13). They killed their own brother (Gen. 4:8). The innocent earth's blood (Gen. 4:10) revealed it to its Maker (thy brother's blood cryeth unto me from the ground). The very earth, the soil of America, soaked with the innocent blood of the so-called Negroes shed by this race devils, now cryeth out to its Maker for her burden of carrying the innocent blood of the righteous slain upon her. Let us take a look at the devils creation from the teaching of the Holy Qur-an.

"And when your Lord said to the angels, I am going to place in the earth one who shall rule, the angels said: "What will Thou place in it such as shall make mischief in it and shed blood, we celebrate Thy praise and extol Thy holiness" (Holy Qur-an Sharrieff 2:30)

This devil race has and still is doing just that—making mischief and shedding blood of the black nation whom they were grafted from. (MTBM pg. 128)

Holy Qur-an 2:45

Patience and Prayer

2:45 "And seek assistance through patience and prayer, and this is hard except for the humble ones,"

Holy Qur-an 40:5

People of Noah reject Messenger

40:5 Before them the people of Noah and the parties after them rejected (prophets), and every nation purposed against its messenger to destroy him, and disputed by means of falsehood to render null thereby the truth, so I seized them; how (terrible) was then My retribution!

It is Allah who taught me this is a race of devils, and those of you who think yourselves to be theologians Know they are a race of devils according to the scriptures. Some of you may argue that you do not believe the scriptures where they teach the Knowledge of this race of people, but this is written in both the Holy Qur-an and Bible several times. You will be punished for ignoring this truth as were the Israelites. They were in love with the Egyptians who were jealous and envious of Moses. The wisdom of Jehovah was Israelite. The Egyptians opposed Moses, and Allah became angry as the Bible teaches you. He, therefore, sent fiery and angry serpents to fight and kill those who were rebelling against Moses' leadership. So it is with you today.

> *Before them, the people of Noah and the parties after them rejected [prophet]), and every nation purposed against its messenger to destroy him, and disputed by means of falsehood to render null thereby the truth, so I seized them; how[terrible] was then My retribution!" Holy Qur-an 40:05*

The fifth verse is a warning to us today. It speaks of people God has marked for destruction. Your actions are the same as disbelievers before you. They made mockery of Allah's Messenger and designed plans against him. They planned to destroy him, just as the present day disbelievers plan against my life. They desire to destroy me (the present Messenger).

How terrible was Allah's disapproval of their actions against His Messenger; so it is today. *(MTBM pg. 208)*

Holy Qur-an 5:3

Perfected for you

> *5:3 Forbidden to you is that which dies of itself, and blood, and flesh of swine, and that on which any other name than that of Allah has been invoked, and the strangled (animal) and that beaten to death, and that killed by a fall, and that killed by goring with the horn, and that which wild beasts have eaten-except what you slaughter; and that which is sacrificed on stones set up (for idols), and that you seek to divide by the arrows; that is a transgression. This day have those who disbelieve despaired of your religion, so fear them not, and fear Me. This day have I perfected for you your religion and completed My favour on you and chosen for you Islam as a religion. But whoever is compelled by hunger, not inclining willfully to sin, then surely Allah is Forgiving, Merciful.*

Islam comes after everything else fails. Its significance is the making of Peace. The Muslim's greeting to each other is "Peace." What better religion could we desire after being divided and made enemies of each other? Do not tell us that you have "unity and peace" in the white race's religion called Christianity. The white race does not like Islam, because it is truth and entire submission to the will of Allah, and this is against their nature. They cannot live the life of freedom, justice and equality—not even among themselves.

Many of you sing that old song, "Give Me That Old Time Religion." Islam is that "old time religion." It is as old as God Himself, and God is the Author of Islam. Islam was not invented as is the case of Christianity and other religions. Islam came with Allah (God) and the universe. In the Holy Qur-it says: "This day I have perfected for you, your religion and completed my favour on you; and have chosen for you, Islam as a religion" Holy Qur-an (5:3).

Here, Islam claims to be a perfect religion and its author, the Perfect One (God). What can be imperfect about Islam when it means "Entire submission to the Will of God?" What can be wrong or imperfect about this religion Islam, which was the religion of Noah, Abraham, Moses, Jesus and all the prophets of God, to Muhammad, the last of the Prophets? Islam proves that its author is God, inasmuch as Allah (God) is on the side of every true Muslim. This is easy to see today. Everyone of you who are accepting Islam can bear witness that, for the first time in your life, you feel the power and help of Almighty Allah (God) on your side. Your whole life becomes changed for the better. Your fear is removed. Your grief is gone. Your desire to continue to do evil things is leaving you for good. Love for your brother (your people) for the first time is now becoming a reality. It is the aim of Allah (God) in giving Islam to you and me; to unite us; to remove fear, sorrow, sickness, and to bring us into that heavenly life, peace of mind and contentment. *(MTBM pgs. 79-80)*

Holy Qur-an 33:41-43

Prayer is better than sleep

33:41 O you who believe, remember Allah with much remembrance,

33:42 And glorify Him morning and evening.

33:43 He it is Who sends His blessings on you, and (so do) His angels, that He may bring you forth out of utter darkness into the light. And He is ever Merciful to the believers.

Holy Qur-an 33:45, 46

Prophet, sent you as a witness

33:45 O Prophet, surely We have sent thee as a witness, and a bearer of good news and a warner,

33:46 And as an inviter to Allah by His permission, and as a light-giving sun.

THE SIGNIFICANCE OF PRAYER

O you who believe, remember Allah, with much remembering him frequently and glorify Him morning and evening. He it is Who sends His blessings on you, and so do His angels, that He may bring you forth out of utter darkness into the light. And He is merciful to the believers. [Prayer is better than sleep.] (Holy Qur-an 33:41-43)

This alone is salvation, just to be brought out of the darkness of ignorance into the light of the truth. Who is in more need of the truth than the American so-called Negroes who do not have the knowledge of self nor of anyone else, and who love those who hate them and spitefully use them?

"O Prophet, surely we have sent you as a witness and as a bearer of good news and as a warner and as one inviting to Allah by his permission and as a light-giving torch" (Holy Qur-an 33:45,46). Come to success; prayer and obedience to Allah will bring you success. The prayer is recited standing erect with face towards the east with hands raised and declaring to the one God, Allah, that he has turned himself to Allah (God), the originator of the heavens and earth. This prayer and positions are especially designed and worded for those lost sheep (the so-called Negroes) who have been lost from the knowledge of their God and people and now declare that they are turned again to their God, Allah, and are upright to Him.

Imagine a native Muslim who never was lost from Allah and His people in the Holy Land or Holy City, reciting the above prayer. The prayer has been turned into the wrong direction. He is in the west, looking again due east, confessing his faults for going astray from his God and people and declaring that he has been unjust to himself. He confesses his faults and declares that none can grant him protection from his faults but Allah (God). He further asks that evil morals be turned away from him and that he be guided to the best of morals. He is now leaving the infidels of the west who brought him into darkness and pleading to be guided to better morals. Surely we, the so-called Negroes, lost all of our good morals among the enemies of the West. The type of the so-called Negroes is given in many parables of the Bible. In fact, if the Bible is rightly understood, it is referring to none other than the so-called Negroes and their enemies, the chosen people of God to whom the God gave the firstborn (convert), and even the (Mahdi) Christ offered His life to restore the so-called Negroes again to their own kind.

But the so-called Negroes are blinded with a picture of the Jews' salvation and cannot see their own selves in prophecy. They should shout with joy over the understanding that God has and is causing me to give them of the Book. ***(MTBM pgs. 136-137)***

Holy Qur-an 29:45

Prayer Keeps one away from evil

> 29:45 *Recite that which has been revealed to thee of the Book and Keep up prayer. Surely prayer keeps (one) away from indecency and evil; and certainly the remembrance of Allah is the greatest (force). And Allah Knows what you do.*

Surely the best way to strive to be upright in a sinful world is to pray continuously to the One True God, whose proper name is Allah, for guidance.

As we are generally sinful and easily yield to temptations, it is only fitting to keep up prayer.

Allah, the One True God, has blessed us with the universe. A sun to shine and brighten up the heavens, giving light for us to see; warmth enabling us to live, and causing vegetation to grow and all life to exist. We reside on the planet through His will, so why should we not pray and continuously thank him for this privilege?

He it is who created the atmosphere for us to breathe. He it is who created all good vegetation for us to eat, plus the fowl and other animals which we partake of daily. He it is who created the beautiful atmosphere in which we live, and which we, with our own hands, mutilate and destroy for lack of proper guidance.

We cannot improve upon the nature in which Allah (God) has created all beautiful things, yet we try. We cannot substitute the original beauty with artificial creations, yet we try. So let us realize the power of Allah, that without Him we cannot exist, and make obedience to Allah through our prayers to Him.

Prayer is obligatory in Islam (the true religion). "And remember Allah's favor upon you and the covenant which He made with you, when you said, "We hear and we obey," and fear Allah.

Surely Allah knows well what is in our minds. *(MTBM pg. 135)*

Holy Qur-an 9:63

Punishment sure to overtake hypocrites

> 9:63 *Know they not that whoever opposes Allah and His Messenger, for him is the Fire of hell to abide in it? That is the grievous abasement.*

He (hypocrite) went, first, on the side of the Muslims, and then on the side of the devils and again on the side of the Muslims and against the devils. He is as the Holy Qur-an says—neither this nor that. His greatest desire is for someone to declare him as their leader. He is insane—for leadership and disgrace himself for that office. As I have repeatedly taught—and the scholars and scientists will agree with me the so-called Negro must have divine leadership today. The leader must be divinely appointed, not self-made or made by the people. This is universally known; I am that man, divinely appointed by Allah.

According to the Bible and Holy Qur-an, punishment is sure to overtake hypocrites and those who seek to oppose Allah and His Apostle. I quote here a verse from the Holy Qur-an.

> *"Do they not know that whoever acts in opposition to Allah and His Apostle he shall surely have the fire of hell to abide in it, that is the grievous abasement" (Holy Qur-an 9:63).*

That is the hell that the hypocrites and disbelievers will suffer, and it begins with their feeling of fear and excitement—fear that someone is going to harm those they oppose. There is no fear for this grief of the hypocrites, according to the Holy Qur-an , prostrates them and makes them wish that they were dead. They even wish for someone to kill them.

But Allah, the Holy Qur-an says, will not permit anyone to kill them, because death would take them out of their chastisement and grief. They will now bow in submission to the will of Allah and obedience in following His Messenger, and after a year or so under this condition, they are classified with the devil, to be destroyed in hell-fire—the final end to both. *(MTBM pgs. 262-263)*

Holy Qur-an 89:27-30

Return to your land

89:27 *O soul that art rest,*

89:28 *Return to thy Lord, well-pleased, well-pleasing,*

89:29 *So enter among My servants,*

89:30 *And enter My Garden!*

The life in the hereafter is an image of the spiritual state in this life. Just think how good you feel when in the Divine Spirit for a while. You are so happy; that you don't feel even the pain of sickness, no trouble or sorrow, and that is the way you will feel always in the next life.

We, the so-called Negroes who accept Allah and Islam will reap this glorious joy and happiness. You will be clothed in silk interwoven with gold and eat the best of food that you desire. This is the time when you enter such life for your God is here in person, and you will never be that which you cannot be any more, after believing in Him. My people have been deceived by the hereafter. They think the hereafter is a life of spirits up somewhere in the sky, while it is only on the earth, and you won't change to any spirit beings. The life in the hereafter is only a continuation of the present life. You will be flesh and blood. You won't see spooks coming up out of graves to meet God.

No already physically dead person will be in the hereafter; that is slavery belief, taught to slaves to keep them under control. This is taught also so that they won't be thinking about the wealth of their slave-masters while under the salve-master. The slave is made to believe this will come after death, and his master knows that death settles all, and that you can't return to tell him whether he lied or told the truth. *(MTBM pg. 304)*

Holy Qur-an 30:43

Right Religion

30:43 Then set thyself, being upright, to the right religion before there come from Allah the day which cannot be averted: on that day they will be separated.

ISLAM, THE TRUE RELIGION OF GOD PART II

> *"Set yourself upright to the right religion before there comes from Allah the day which cannot be averted; on that day they shall become separated." (Holy Qur-an 30:43)*

We are now living in the time mentioned above according to the Holy Qur-an. When we as a people should begin setting our faces upright to the religion in the right state and stop believing in the slave-master's slavery religious teachings, which are not in the right state, then we shall be successful and the world will respect us.

Which one of these emblems represent a good religion, the cross or the Star and Crescent? To attract one to do good, you must have something of good. Our religion, Islam, has the best sign (the Crescent). There is no doubt about it. We have taken the best of everything for our own (the Sun, Moon and Stars); ever since it was created by our Father, we know the best. What can be more essential to our well-being than the Sun, Moon, and Stars?

The spiritual meaning of our emblem (the Crescent) is Freedom, Justice, and Equality, not that we "say" one thing and do otherwise; a Muslim tries to carry into practice what he preaches; not so the Christians. They "say" and do not. But after all, their religious emblem (the cross) and its meaning compare with the nature of the so-called Christians. By nature they are murderers. By nature they love to make slaves of others. By nature they are haters of the Black Nation, which loves freedom, justice and equality. It looks strange to see people accepting the cross as a sign of good religion.

The Ten Commandments which Moses gave to them (the white race) have never been practiced by them or those whom they teach. They (the white race) were condemned by Jesus as not obeying. Why should we be looking and begging for that which is good (freedom, justice and equality)! Islam is that right religion (which by nature they cannot give us).

According to the Holy Qur-an (30:30), one of the greatest teachings of brotherhood is laid down by us by the Prophet Muhammad in these words: "A Muslim is not a Muslim until he loves for his brother what he loves for himself." The old Christian religion has been the white man's whip to lash the black man ever since it was organized. My people here in America are fast awakening to the slavery teachings of Christianity to the dislike of their enemies.

A few years ago the so-called Negroes could easily be frightened and worked up into emotion by the preacher, yelling and spitting out foam all over the pulpit, preaching hellfire after death and the dying of Jesus on the cross. He would paint an imaginary picture in the minds of the listeners—of meeting some dead relative up in the heavens (sky) after death or mourn them into grief and sorrow. My people are leaving and rejecting such nonsense as they advance more and more educationally. After they have heard the truth of it all, that Allah has and is teaching me, they will not go near that slavery teaching. Their eyes must be opened to the truth at any price. ***(MTBM pgs. 78-79)***

Chapter 8

Holy Qur-an 4:163 164

Scripture same as revealed

> 4:163 *Surely We have revealed to thee as We revealed to Noah and the prophets after him, and We revealed to Abraham and Ishmael and Isaac and Jacob and the tribes, and Jesus and Job and Jonah and Aaron and Solomon, and We gave to David a scripture."*
>
> 4:164 *And (We sent) messengers We have mentioned to you before and messengers We have not mentioned to you. And to Moses Allah addressed His word, speaking (to him) –*

Man makes himself a fool to try attacking Him in arguments. So, we have no doubt the Holy Qur-an is from the Lord of the Worlds. It is one of the cleanest reading books you ever read. The God that revealed the Holy Qur-an Sharrieff to Muhammad is the same that revealed the scriptures to the other prophets according to the Holy Qur-an Sharrieff, "Surely we have revealed to you as we revealed to Noah and the prophets after him, we revealed to Abraham, Ishmael, Isaac, Jacob, the Tribes, Jesus, Job, Jonah, Aaron, Solomon and we gave to David a scripture, and Moses Allah addressed His words speaking to Him. And we sent Apostles we have mentioned to you before, and Apostles we have not mentioned to you" (4:163, 164). Some people whom the devils have deceived in regard to the Holy Qur-an call it the work of Muhammad.

Some call the religion Islam a dream of Muhammad, though the Bible doesn't say it is from God, but the prophets, and is dedicated to King James of England. The white race does not like to worship a black god and his prophets. They are too proud to recognize a black prophet or god. The so-called Negroes should know this by this time. The Holy Qur-an's readings are not the kind that will lull one to sleep, but to get a real Qur-an one should know the Arabic language in which it is written. However, you can find a good translation of it by Yusuf Ali and Muhammad Ali. *(MTBM pgs. 92-93)*

Holy Qur-an 16:36

Shun the devil

> 16:36 *And certainly We raised in every nation a messenger, saying: serve Allah and shun the devil. Then of them was he whom Allah guided and of them was he whose remaining in error was justly due. So travel in the land, then see what was the end of the rejectors.*

We have thousands of the darker people joining Islam all over the earth, but a very few whites accept Islam. The door of Islam has never been open to everyone who desired to accept it, but today it is different. The door of this religion is now being closed against the white race which has repeatedly rejected Islam, made mockery of it, persecuted and killed the Prophets and the believers (the followers), hid and concealed the truth of it and its God, Allah, who is the God of the Universe, and Islam, His only religion. They follow the poor teacher of Islam seeking a way or an excuse to kill him. They put spies (stool pigeons) on him to try to find a way to charge him with something other than the truth in order to do him evil for the truth's sake that he teaches.

As David says in his Psalms 94:20: "Shall the throne of iniquity have fellowship with thee, which frameth mischief by a law?" The poor lost-found members of the Tribe of Shabazz (nicknamed "Negroes" by their slave-masters) can well understand that they are the victims of such a frame up against them throughout America when they seek truth, love and unity among themselves. The white race does not want to see the poor black people of America united in Islam, a religion that is of Allah (God) backed by the spirit and power of God, to unite all of its believers into one nation of brotherhood. It is the only unifying religion known and tried by the races and nations of earth. This the white race knows.

They were offered Islam by Musa (Moses), Jesus, Muhammad and many other prophets, but they rejected it. "And certainly we raised in every nation an Apostle saying serve Allah and shun the devil. So there were others against whom error was due; therefore, travel in the land, then see what was the end of the rejectors" (Holy Qur-an 16:36). The prophets had delivered to them the message of truth and shown them the right way; but they chose to remain in error (evil doings). This stands true of this people today. They know the truth, and right from wrong but they like wrong or evil better than right; therefore, they are against Islam and its truth. The Holy Qur-an says:

"Surely we have revealed to you as we revealed to Noah and the Prophets after him, and we revealed to Abraham and Ishmael and the Tribes, and Jesus, Job and Jonah, Aaron, Solomon, and we gave to David a scripture. We sent Apostles as the givers of good news and as warners, so that people should not have a plea against Allah after the coming of the Apostles" (4:163, 165). The Messengers of Allah (God) bring good news to the people but if that good news is rejected, therefore, they are warned that bad news will come.

The Christian white world, whose leader and teacher is the Pope of Rome (the Father of the church) claims that Jesus brought a new religion to them. But the scripture of both Bible and Holy Qur-an denies such false charge, and makes Jesus' religion the same as the Prophets' who were before Him. Muhammad was also given the same religion of Jesus and the Prophets before Him. ***(MTBM pgs. 131-132)***

Holy Qur-an 2:112

Submit to Allah

2:112 Nay, whoever submits himself entirely to Allah and he is the doer of good (to others), he has his reward from his Lord, and there is no fear for such nor shall they grieve.

Islam, the religion of entire submission to the will of Allah (God). "Nay, whoever submits his whole self to Allah and is a doer of good, he will get his regard with his Lord, on such shall be no fear, nor shall they grieve." (Holy Qur-an 2:112).

That and that alone is Salvation according to the Holy Qur-an . Fear is the number one enemy that is blocking progress to the so-called Negroes of America. This fear causes them to grieve. The whole world knows the poor so-called Negroes of America have suffered and still suffer more grief and sorrow than any people on the earth! This fear is the fear of the slave master (white man) and what the slave-masters dislike. Let the so-called Negroes submit to Allah (God) and they will not fear anymore, nor will they grieve. As it is written: "The fear of man bringeth a snare." (Proverbs 29:25) It has surely snared the so-called Negroes.

The Lord of the Worlds Finder of we the lost members of the Asiatic Black Nation for 400 years said that the slave-masters put fear in our Fathers when they were babies. Allah is the only one that can remove this fear from us but he will not remove it from us until we submit to His will, not our will, and fear Him and Him alone. Then, as it is written, "And it shall come to pass in the day that the Lord shall give thee rest from sorrow and from thy fear, and from the hard bondage wherein thou was made to serve" (Isaiah 14:3). There are so many places that I could point out in the Bible & Holy Qur-an that warn us of fearing our enemies above or equal to the fear of Allah (God). It is a fool who has greater fear of the devils (white man) than Allah who has the power to destroy the devils and their power to their followers (Rev. 21:8; Holy Qur-an 7:18 and 15:43). *(MTBM pgs. 29-30)*

Holy Qur-an 3:82

Submit to Allah

3:82 Seek they then other than Allah's religion? And to Him submits whoever is in the heavens and the earth, willingly or unwillingly, and to Him they will be returned.

The Christians go to war against each other daily, killing their own brothers and others. The righteous must be rid of such people. Make Islam to overcome all other religions whether the disbelievers like it or not. Our God is One God. Can One God believe in more than one religion and be true to Himself and others?

If the other religions were true religions, surely Allah (God) would not send an apostle to overcome them with another religion. "Is it other than Allah's religion that they seek to follow and to Him submit whoever is in the heavens and earth, willingly or unwillingly" (Holy Qur-an 3:82). We all bear witness to the truth that everything of Allah's creation obeys Him, regardless of size or numbers.

But the proud, wicked man of sin refuses to submit and goes about teaching ignorant people not to believe in Allah and His religion, Islam. *(MTBM pg. 77)*

Holy Qur-an 30:43

They will be separated

30:43 Then set thyself, being upright, to the right religion before there come from Allah the day which cannot be averted: On that day they will be separated.

We read of the history of the flood that drowned a disobedient people who refuse to take warnings from Allah's prophet, Noah.

The following verse warns you and me, the so-called American Negroes, that after nearly one hundred years we have not been able to see that Christianity is not an upright religion; and it further warns us that on that day we will be separated. These days now approach you and me, SO MAKE A DECISION. (Holy Qur-an 30:43) ***(MTBM pg. 143)***

Holy Qur-an 2:2

This Book No doubt

> *2:2 This book, there is no doubt in it, is a guide to those who keep their duty.*

THE BIBLE AND HOLY QUR-AN: WHICH ONE CONTAINS WORDS OF GOD? Both books are called holy. The word of Allah (God) is holy, and His word is true. Therefore, all truth is holy; for Allah (God) is holy and is the author of truth, without the shadow of a doubt! Allah is the representative of the Holy Qur-an (not a prophet) in these words: "This book, there is no doubt of it is a guide to those who guard against evil" (2:2), translated by Maulvi Muhammad Ali. Abdullah Yusuf Ali's translation of the same verse reads nearly the same: "This is the book; in it is guidance, sure without doubt to those who fear Allah (God)" (2:2). ***(MTBM pg. 86)***

Holy Qur-an 3:18

True religion

> *3:18 Surely the (true) religion with Allah is Islam. And those to who were given the book differed only after knowledge had come to them, out of envy among themselves. And whoever disbelieves in the messages of Allah Allah indeed is quick in reckoning.*

The true religion of Allah (God) is Islam (Holy Qur-an 3:18) The emblem of Islam represents the sun, moon and stars; the meaning is Freedom (Sun), Justice (Star), and Equality (Moon).

No other nation's religion has the sun, moon, and stars as its emblem. No religion is worthwhile if its roots are not found in the universal order of things. No nation can use the sun, moon and stars to represent their government or religion but the nation that owns it (the nation of Islam).

We are the sole owners of the earth. It was our father who made it. The prayer service of Islam is not equaled by any other religion five prayers a day made the face turned in the direction of the sunrise.

Prayer is at sunrise, noon, mid-afternoon, sundown and before returning. On awakening during the night, another prayer is made. In fact, two prayers should be said during the night, making a total of seven prayers a day. There is no worship of a Sunday or Sabbath in Islam. All the days are worship days. The Muslims wash and clean all exposed parts of their bodies before prayer early at the gray dawn of day. *(MTBM pg. 77)*

Holy Qur-an Chapter 18:

Turned into apes and swine

You have learned, from the reading of history, that a nation's permanent success depends on its obedience to Allah. We have seen the white race (devils) in heaven, among the righteous, causing trouble (making mischief and causing bloodshed), until they were discovered.

They made trouble for six months, right in heaven, deceiving the ancient original people who were holy. But, when they learned just who was causing the trouble; they, as you have learned, cast the troublemakers out into the worst and poorest part of our planet earth.

They were punished by being deprived of divine guidance, for 2,000 years which brought them almost into the family of wild beasts -- going upon all fours; eating raw and unseasoned, uncooked food; living in caves and treetops, climbing and jumping from one tree to the other.

Even today, they like climbing and jumping. The monkeys are from them. Before their time, there were no such things as monkeys, apes and swine. Read the Holy Qur-an (Chapter 18) entitled: "The Cave" The Holy Qur-an mentions them as being turned into apes and swine as a divine curse, because of their disbelief in Moses.

We do know that both of these animals are loved and befriended by the white race, along with the dog. But, all of the divine curses sent upon the white race in these days are not enough to serve as a warning to that race. They rose up from the caves and hillsides of Europe, went back to Asia, and have ruled nine-tenths of that great continent.

Muhammad set the devils back for 1000 years. They were released on the coming of Columbus, and his finding of this Western Hemisphere. They have been here now over 400 years. Their worst and most unpardonable sins were the bringing of the so-called Negroes here to do their labor.

The so-called Negroes have not only given free labor, but have given their lives on the soil of their masters and all over the earth wherever his hateful and murdering slave-master wants them to go. Now, the slave wants better treatment. They are fast learning today, that these are the children of those who made merchandise out of their fathers. The devil is the "devil" regardless of place and time. ***(MTBM pgs. 103-104)***

Holy Qur-an 53:57-62

53:57 *The near event draws nigh*

53:58 *There is none besides Allah to remove it.*

53:59 *Wonder you then at this announcement?*

53:60 *And do you laugh and not weep,*

53:61 *While you sport?*

53:62 *So bow down in prostration before Allah and serve (Him).*

Holy Qur-an 40:4-6

40:4 None dispute concerning the messages of Allah but those who disbelieve, so let not their control in the land deceive thee.

40:5 Before them the people of Noah and the parties after them rejected (prophets), and every nation purposed against its messenger to destroy him, and disputed by means of falsehood to render null thereby the truth, so I seized them; how (terrible) was then My retribution!

40:6 And thus did the word of thy Lord prove true against those who disbelieve that they are the companions of the Fire.

THE GREAT DECISIVE BATTLE IN THE SKY

And there shall be signs in the sun and in the moon and in the stars, and upon the earth distress of nations with perplexity; the sea and the waves roaring; men's hearts failing them for looking after those things which are coming on the earth: for the powers of heaven shall be shaken. They see the Son of Man coming in a cloud with power and great glory' (St. Luke 21:25-27).

You will bear me witness that we are living in such time as mentioned in the above prophecy -- signs in the sun and in the moon. The phenomena going on in the sun and its family of planets testify to the truth that something of the greatest magnitude is about to take place. The final war or battle between God and the devils in the sky.

Allah (God) who has power over all things, is bringing the powers of the sun, moon and stars into display against His enemies. The fire of the sun to scorch and burn men and the vegetation and dry up the waters. The moon will eclipse her light to bring darkness upon man and upon all living things, to disrupt with her waves all air communications. The magnetic powers of the moon will bring about such tidal waves of seas and oceans as man has never witnessed before: the sea and waves roaring.

As men's hearts fail them with fear at the sea, looking upon great tidal waves coming toward them like mountains, they also shall see such a great display of power from Allah (God) in the sky that their hearts will fail. Great earthquakes never felt before since man was upon the earth will take place, say the Bible and the Holy Qur-an. The Holy Qur-an says: "There will not be one city left that will not be leveled to the ground." Using this force against the enemies of Allah will make it impossible for them to survive.

This all known to this world, but why are they trying to build up a defense against God. It is useless. America has it coming. Look how she has been and still is mistreating her freed slaves (so-called Negroes). The foolish (so-called) Negro preachers and leaders want social equality with these, their enemies. The great distress of nations spoken or prophesied of coming in the above chapter and verses is now going on. Confusion, confusion all over the Western world today.

They (devils) see the end of their world and they see the signs of the Son of Man coming in the sky with power and great glory (the great Ezekiel's wheel and the unity of the Muslim world and the distress of nations).

The so-called Negro must awaken before it is too late. They think the white man's Christianity will save them regardless of what happens, and they are gravely mistaken. They must know that the white man's religion is not from God nor from Jesus or any other of the prophets. It is controlled by the white race and not by Almighty Allah (God).

"The ever approaching draws nigh, there shall be none besides Allah to remove it. Do you wonder at this announcement? And will you laugh and not weep? While you sport and play, so make obeisance to Allah and serve Him" (Holy Qur-an 53:57, 58, 59, 60). Let us remember another Qur-an saying: "None disputes concerning the communications of Allah (God) but those who disbelieve, therefore let not their going to and fro in the cities deceive you. The people of Noah and the parties after them rejected prophets before them, and every nation purposed against their Apostle to destroy him, and they disputed by means of the falsehood that they might thereby render null the truth. Therefore I destroyed them: how was then my retribution and thus did the word of your Lord prove true against those who disbelieved that they are the inmates of the fire" (Holy Qur-an 40:4-6). *(MTBM pgs. 292-293)*

THE END

The Holy Qur'an The Quranic verses and commentary cited in this work are taken from:

- The Holy Qur'an: Arabic Text, English Translation and Commentary by Maulana Muhammad Ali. Published by Ahmadiyya Anjuman Isha'at Islam Lahore Inc., 1994.

Message to the Blackman in America Additional insights and foundational teachings are referenced from:

- Message to the Blackman in America by the Honorable Elijah Muhammad. Copyright 1965, published by Muhammad's Temple No. 2.

About The Author

Elijah Muhammad *(1897-1975) - Leader of the Nation of Islam and Advocate for Black Empowerment* Elijah Muhammad led the Nation of Islam (NOI), transforming it into a major movement for Black self-reliance and economic empowerment. Born in Georgia, he migrated to Detroit, where he met NOI founder Wallace Fard Muhammad in 1931. After Fard's disappearance, he took leadership in 1934, promoting Black nationalism, self-sufficiency, and religious discipline. Under his guidance, the NOI built businesses, schools, and farms, influencing figures like Malcolm X, Muhammad Ali, and Louis Farrakhan. Despite government persecution, he expanded the NOI's reach, leaving a lasting impact on Black empowerment and religious movements.

Last God of the Old World and First God of the New World Hereafter.

www.ingramcontent.com/pod-product-compliance
Ingram Content Group UK Ltd.
Pitfield, Milton Keynes, MK11 3LW, UK
UKHW021432280726
14060UKWH00001BA/29